W9-BSA-985

PATHS AND WALKWAYS

Simple Projects, Contemporary Designs

A GARDEN DESIGN BOOK

PATHS AND WALKWAYS

Simple Projects, Contemporary Designs

HAZEL WHITE

Photography by Matthew Plut

CHRONICLE BOOKS
SAN FRANCISCO

Dedicated to:

My sister Sandra (HW)

Stan and Yolanda (MP)

✧⟩⟩⟩⟩⟩⟩⟩⟩⟩⟩⟩⟩⟩⟩⟩⟩⟩⟩⟩⟩⟩⟩✧

Text copyright © 1998 by Hazel White.
Photographs copyright © 1998 by Matthew Plut.
All rights reserved. No part of this book may be
reproduced in any form without written permis-
sion from the publisher.

Library of Congress
Cataloging-in-Publication Data:
White, Hazel.
Paths and walkways: simple projects, contem-
porary designs / Hazel White; photography by
Matthew Plut.
p. cm.
"A garden design book."
Includes bibliographical references (p.) and index.
ISBN 0-8118-1429-7 (pb)
1. Garden walks—Amateurs' manuals. I. Title.
TH4970.W45 1998

712—dc21   97-6980
CIP

Printed in Hong Kong.

Designed and typeset by David Bullen Design.

Distributed in Canada by Raincoast Books
8680 Cambie Street
Vancouver, British Columbia V6P 6M9

10 9 8 7 6 5 4 3 2 1

Chronicle Books
85 Second Street
San Francisco, California 94105

Web Site: www.chronbooks.com

CONTENTS

INTRODUCTION

Paths throw the garden open to exploration. They set people into motion. The eye sees a path heading away somewhere and the feet follow, irresistibly, out from the house into the elements on a journey to the depths of the garden, even if that's only ten yards away.

Flower gardeners will steer a path through the old-fashioned fragrance of midnight-blue and white sweet peas that bloom by the fence. Anyone who loves fall woodlands may swing a path under a ginkgo tree, just to be able to stand at the end of a cold November day ankle deep in a blanket of tiny gold fans and watch the last few spin down to the ground. An artist may take a path past stone-carved heads sleeping on a bank, then under blue glass bottles in the treetops shining bright against the sky. The garden is revealed in this way, by degrees, from paths connecting one beautiful point to another.

In walking perhaps a hundred garden paths for this book, I realized that the most enchanting gardens are built by people who've learned not to be coy about what they find beautiful. They've edged their paths with blond boulders streaked with a red mineral that exactly matches the red of the barberry leaves; or with football-sized chunks of cloudy blue-green slag glass, which shoot specks of light into the shade under the trees. They've laid out grand flagstone paths to connect the terrace and the pool, but they've also laid paths to the places where they like to linger—perhaps it's the woodpile sheltered by a tin roof, a raked gray gravel path butting the mossy sawed logs, with a chair right there to watch the rain slant across the garden and drip from the tin. Perhaps it's at the top of a steep bank, reachable only in a goatlike scramble up a ladder of stepping-stones, but worth the view of the river through a break in the pines.

I grew up in an English farmhouse garden with no path to speak of. The rutted gravel driveway came up past the brick-walled vegetable garden and swung in through iron gates to the front door. Gardening, to my father, was a chore like other farm chores. Plain lawn stretched out on two sides of the house, bounded by a ring of tilting crabapple trees. In the back, Brussels sprouts and potatoes grew in long, straight rows, a few rows halting short at the corner, around the abandoned greenhouse.

I reached the greenhouse on a strip of grass under the pear trees against the wall, a permanent strip beyond the reach of the tractor and plow that turned over the vegetable garden each fall. I'd slip around the outhouse, past the scarlet rhubarb thrusting through its chimney pot cover, through a tunnel of bees hazing the pear trees and flying up from the fruit spoiling in the grass. In summer, the path was hedged with rows of kidney beans hanging over tall crossed beech sticks. I could amble then, unseen, picking a pear and tossing it into the beans because it was tart, saving the moment of arriving at the musty warm greenhouse.

On a different continent now, and in a small urban house, the path in my garden that I like the most goes out through nasturtiums under three birch trees. There, beams of cool green light filter onto the path, and yellow finches bounce the branches, snatching catkin seed.

But paths have plain work to do too. They get visitors from the road to the front door safely in all weathers. They get children from the house to the pool quickly. They get the wheelbarrow from the garden to the toolshed or the garbage area, without it tipping over in a rut. They get people off the back porch and across the lawn to the place where the view is best and the breeze blows.

The pleasure of building paths is to combine function and art. All the paths in this book will transport people comfortably from place A to place B—on soft cool grass, deep, clicking gravel, formal cut flagstone, concrete pavers, or pocked pink brick. They were planned by garden designers and landscape architects. They are contemporary, American, and many are from award-winning gardens.

If you're starting a new garden, or remodeling your garden, look through the first chapter, "Designing Paths." Paths have a special role to play in making gardens work well; the secrets of path design are in that chapter. The next chapter, "Building Paths," describes the practical business of path construction: tools, buying paving materials and plants, a proper base for different climates, suggestions for building a path on a slope.

The path "recipes," in the chapters that follow, contain all the information you need: lists of tools, materials, and plants, and the how-to steps for creating each path. The paths are all easy to build. The ones categorized as moderately difficult merely contain more steps than the others, or require more attention to detail or a certain level of confidence. If you've never handled a brick or a trowel, there's no need to summon false courage; some of the recipes that are simple and least expensive to build are also the most beautiful.

Even in the smallest garden, there's room for a simple path and a simple destination, perhaps five strides on pavers to a makeshift seat with a space at your feet for a coffee cup. If you plant fragrant plants around the seat or place a piece of outdoor sculpture there, you'll have signaled a sense of arrival. The garden expands in the imagination that way. There's a place to head out to, an outdoor space to live in for a few minutes every day.

DESIGNING PATHS

Paths give a garden structure. In a place packed with flowers and compost piles and berries and lawns and leaves and ornaments and vegetables and containers—paths take you kindly by the elbow and guide you through. If the paths are well designed, once you leave the house behind, you'll only see it again in its best light, you'll recognize the way to the summerhouse, never catching a glimpse of the turn to the garbage cans, and you'll be visually surprised, lulled, and delighted all the way to the bottom of the garden and back. This chapter explains the secrets of great path design.

PATHS AS GARDEN BONES ≈≈≈ From the chateau at Vaux-le-Vicomte, outside Paris, straight lines of topiary cones, boxwood parterres, and gravel paths roll out in military precision to a grand spectacle of water jets and statuary on the horizon. The main walkway is as broad and directional as a street; at right angles to it run two cross-axes, with smaller paths ending in smaller water features. In winter, the gardens are flowerless and the trees a treillage of gray twigs instead of hoods of fresh green, but the effect is no less dramatic. The main path draws one out across the wide open terraces into the spray of fountain water; the cross-paths offer the shelter of hedges along quiet canals into the woods.

A simple symmetrical layout of paths works well in small gardens too. The garden can be filled out and ornamented with stone urns, a water feature, and myriad shades of green foliage, as at Vaux-le-Vicomte, or decorated cottage-style with birdhouses and flowers that thread through the trees, tumble over the hedges, and push up between the paving stones. The decoration can even change from year to year. But the paths, the bones, are vital because they organize the space, lead people into and through it, from one area to the next.

Symmetry may not suit your taste, the architecture of your home, or the surrounding landscape—especially if you live in the country among rolling hills or your garden slopes this way and that and won't hold a symmetrical pattern without leveling and terracing. But without some kind of structure the garden will feel confusing.

Designer Harland Hand structures his gardens informally, to be experienced in the same way as we experience nature—from trails that lead toward shelters and lookouts. In his own half-acre sloping garden, a concrete path winds around outcrops of rock and down across screes of flowers, broadens into mini-terraces, or shelters, which contain a bench or a small pond, and on from shelter to shelter to the overlook, a view of the San Francisco Bay. The path then turns back toward the house, climbing up the slope past other resting places to the starting point.

On the design plan, the path shows clearly as the main organizing element of the garden, a large loop with the mini-terraces positioned at different angles to the path to offer views across, down, and back up the garden. There's not a straight line on the plan, and instead of large architectural blocks of just a few plants, as at Vaux-le-Vicomte, literally thousands of different plants, often just one of each, decorate this garden. Yet the path holds the garden together just as cleverly as at Vaux-le-Vicomte. It cuts a broad swath of air and light through Harland's dizzying collection of orchids, succulents, and azaleas, leading one reliably on from place to place, revealing everything by degrees.

DESTINATIONS ⋙ In designer Sharon Osmond's garden, the deck adjoining the kitchen reveals most of her tiny city yard. There's little reason to leave the deck; a pergola shades the cushioned willow armchairs, and sculpture and flowers are within arm's reach. But the eye keeps locking onto a creamy opalescent globe radiating like a beacon atop a blue column at the edge of the garden. It's partially hidden by shrubs, but is probably the destination of the path that bends away from the deck. Always the eye notices first, then the feet follow. Turning the corner in the short path, six strides from the deck, the column comes into full view, and the path broadens slightly and ends in a circle full of surprises: the globe up close is an antique lamp sitting on a silver tray; a Kashmir cypress, soft as lace, weeps to its base; and a chair invites you to stay a while in this tiny garden within the garden.

If you've laid a path into the garden, you've extended an invitation to take someone somewhere. When no hint of the destination can be seen from the starting point of the path, entice people toward it by placing a strong visual marker at the path entrance—a plinth-shaped boulder and a skinny Italian cypress or an engraved stone that announces a special kind of journey. A plain threshold stone, large and welcoming, announces the start of the path more subtly.

A path may end at any focal point. Among the best are a sudden view through an iron gate out across the countryside, an arbor heavy with fragrant old roses, a statue with an inscription or fine carving, a fountain with a bowl for trailing one's hands through spray and cool water, a planter of strawberries, or a seat tucked back into rustling foliage for shelter and privacy. What these elements have in common is that they offer an experience that can't be had from a distance. They affect one's senses and change one's mood, generous rewards for walking the path.

TENSION AND MYSTERY ALONG THE WAY ⚹⚹⚹

One day I will travel to the imperial villa of Shugaku-in in Kyoto to walk the path to the teahouse on the top of the hill. In their book, *A Guide to the Gardens of Kyoto*, Marc Treib and Ron Herman describe the tension that builds as one climbs to the summit. From the flat, open rice fields, a gravel path heads around the hill and up through a broad avenue of dark pines planted equidistantly and rhythmically (I can see the alternating bars of light and shadow across the gravel). At the thatched imperial gate, under a huge tree canopy, the path pauses where one formally enters the teahouse garden. It resumes as stepping-stones set between close, towering hedges, which make a dim, narrow tunnel. The path turns and climbs around the hillside in the dark until it suddenly bursts out into the sunlight on the summit: "The guest faces the tea house and senses a presence behind him. Turning, a vast panorama is revealed. Trees, woods, a reflecting lake, and in the distance, a superb vista of the mountains. . . . Although the view would be magnificent under any conditions, it is overwhelming [after] the confined approach."

In a residential garden a path through a tunnel of vines on arches ending in a splash of light on an urn gives a similar sense of tension and surprise. So does a damp forget-me-not path, shaded between a high boundary fence and a steep bank, when it suddenly climbs into the light alongside a fountain of creamy, sweet, mock orange blossoms. Running a path through a narrow point in a trellis or hedge, turning it out of sight around a corner where a pink phormium glows in late afternoon light, across planks over a drainage ditch, under an arch: these points on the way create anticipation and mystery, drawing people on through the garden.

In the calm spaces along the path, perhaps where you want to slow people down to notice individual plants, provide stopping places. Widen the path into a tiny terrace with a table and two chairs, set a bench off from the path, wedge a stone slab deep into a bank and make a backrest out of a piece of cornice from the salvage yard. Furnish these mini-destinations with a fragrant shrub or a tub of water, or site them to show off a glimpse of a distant view (a path to this spot is essential if there's no view from the house). Save the fireworks, though, for the grand destination at the path's end or, if it's a circular path, at the farthest point from the house, where it begins to turn back.

The simplest elements along the path are often the most interesting. Off-the-shelf bridges or gazebos are hard to settle into the garden naturally. Landscape designer Nancy Hammer's award-winning garden in Seattle (see page 63) uses simple repeating square plinths of granite stones to draw the eye along the path toward different areas of the garden. People immediately pick up on the cue and head toward the next one. On a woodland walk in Virginia, the cues are less formal and more varied—an unusual tree, a piece of broken sculpture, a fallen log, a small clearing where sunlight hits the floor. The cues lead one on and on into the wood; the path skirts the clearing, offering only a view of it, but it has worked as a visual marker. The path can even peter out, says Nancy. People will forge a path through waist-high ferns if their eyes have spotted a cue on the other side.

Sound draws people along a path perhaps more reliably than any visual element. At the Bloedel Reserve on Bainbridge Island, Washington, I followed a path far out across a long, hot meadow away from the gardens to discover the source of an erratic but insistent honking. The path at last slipped into a copse of red alder, water came into view, and suddenly there were two trumpeter swans, gliding past a bench on a promontory that ran right out into a lake.

A trickle from a pipe into a bowl will generate enough sound to pull people around a corner or out into the garden from the back door. Bamboo rustling in a breeze or seed pods knocking against bark will also draw people forward along a path through the garden.

STRAIGHT OR CURVED? ≋≋≋

"Straight paths are formal and only suitable for grand spaces; curving paths are more natural, especially in small gardens." This opinion is a prevailing one, but more or less erroneous. The traditional English cottage garden has a straight path from the road to the front door and a straight path from the back door down through the dahlias to the potting shed. The bones are strong, but the effect is casual, because a profusion of flowers loosens the whole thing up. The entrance to the thirty-seven-acre Lotusland estate in Montecito, California, is a grand curve, dramatized and formalized by edges of a single variety of huge agave.

What matters most is the logic and clarity of path shapes. "The stronger and simpler [the] lines they follow the better," wrote the late British designer Russell Page. To be avoided is an "indecisive arrangement . . . a basic error which even the most skillful planting will never be able to put right." Page confessed he found curves harder to manage than straight lines. He often used straight paths close to the house—extending the architectural lines into the garden and anchoring the house to its site—then curving paths nearer to the natural landscape, following the lay of the land, perhaps mimicking the sweep of a distant hill.

In urban gardens, where the natural landscape is a collage of straight streets, rectangular lots, and block buildings, a curve needs to be bold and geometric to look as appropriate as a straight line. Away from the house, especially in a rural environment, paths may wend this way and that as long as they follow nature's logic and turn for a clear reason: to avoid a boulder or a tree or to skirt a pond or a steep drop in the land. A single sweeping curve in a small garden should turn around something: a mass of tall flowers provides reason enough, but a tree is even better because it will partially obscure the view and lead people around the curve.

Paths that meander for no reason immediately register on the mind as irritating. These are the paths drawn out by tossing a flexible hose pipe onto the garden and approving the curves without any reference to the shape of the land or nearby architecture. The hose-pipe method, warns contemporary garden designer John Brookes, leads to a "wiggly wobbly thing." Brookes's method, explained in his *Garden Design Workbook,* is to draw a grid for the garden based on the modules of space on the house facade (architects generally work on a similar grid to ensure that the proportion of the windows relates to the front steps, for example). The paving is worked out on the grid; the curves are derived from arcs of circles that fit into the grid. Nothing ends up little or fiddly. Brookes creates clean, open shapes, curved or straight, "to get a bit of punch in there," and then softens the lines by planting cottage flowers and grasses in the paving.

SMALL GARDENS, GREAT PATHS ⪷⪷⪷ Lay a gravel path

from the back porch across a small lawn toward a seat in a vegetable patch, and there's a place to head out to. In winter, when sunlight breaks through between storms, frost may be sparkling on the tops of the last leeks; maybe a couple of shriveled apples still dot the ground or pink dogwood leaves are catching the light. Without a path there's no invitation to cross the lawn (no *way* to cross it in wet weather) and no visual reminder of that place at the bottom of the garden.

Small gardens seem larger when the eye distinguishes two spaces instead of one. The smallest gardens are ones taken in from the back door in a single glance. Suggest a second space, with a path leading somewhere, and the garden grows in the imagination.

A path of brick or stone continues a hard surface from the house into the garden, opening up the garden as a year-round living space. In a garden too small for a patio, a dining table can be set up across a path, and candles brought out to light the path edges. The entire scene can be dismantled in the morning.

The sharp lines of stone and gravel and brick accentuate the organic shapes of flowers, leaves, bare twigs, moss, seedpods, and grasses. It would be a shame to forgo the textural values of path materials just to save space.

If you're a plant collector and loathe to give up room for a decent path, instead of making do without one, consider reducing the size of the lawn. Place the choicest plants in your collection on either side of the path, in pots and urns at the corners, in the cracks between the paving units. Now that the plants are touchable and truly on display, people will more likely understand your passion; they'll notice that the new bicolored primula matches the neighboring pot, that the hairy stems and bulging buds of the oriental poppy are the exact same milky green as its leaves.

PLANTS IN THE PATH ~~~

Violets, nicotianas, geums, lychnis, and lamb's ears have made their own garden in the concrete side path that runs from my garbage can to the street. They're weeds really, aggressive volunteers that have grown from seeds fallen out of debris. The garbage can is the focal point; over the years, thousands of seeds have burst all about it when I pushed the debris from the flower beds inside. The sweet purple violets bloom faster in the chipped concrete than in the garden proper; they must hurry to seed themselves because they know nutrients are short. When I'm watering the front garden, once in a while I turn the spray toward this upstart garden (I shouldn't really be encouraging the degeneration of the path) and I watch over the hose constantly so that it doesn't swipe down any of the thigh-high nicotianas whose flowers open at twilight, sticky, white, and fragrant.

The effect of nature reclaiming a strip of pavement is so gladdening that it's worth building in as part of the path plan. Make a five-foot-wide path of cut stone in rectangles and squares, formal as can be, and it will lose its rigidity completely if you omit a stone here and there and plant fluffy fragrant thyme or tall mulleins, ornamental grasses, sisyrinchiums, or foxgloves in the spaces. Loose plants like these contrast beautifully with the flat hard-edged stone; as you dodge around them along the path, you can't help but be affected by the sense that nature has forced its way through the floor. A wide swath of gravel, shale, or brick can be loosened up in the same way.

Stepping-stones show off well in a tight-foliaged low ground cover like moss or creeping thyme. Slightly taller plants, like snow-in-summer, will partially obscure the stones. Choose a plant that will withstand some stepping on, though people generally will skip and wobble from step to step rather than tramp on the cracks. A plant with vigorous roots will squeeze out weeds, but too vigorous a plant, such as periwinkle, can be a nuisance around stepping-stones, because it needs frequent hand trimming to prevent it from smothering the path. Dark plants accentuate the shapes of pale stones; gray-foliaged plants soften the shapes.

Miniature bulbs make a luxurious plant for the gaps between closely laid pavers. One species of oxalis produces lovely white trumpet flowers that unfold when the sun strikes the path and roll back into tiny twists as the light passes over. It beats out the weeds, and, in fall, the cloverlike foliage turns amber-rusty. I saw it at the end of a stone terrace, picking up the color of the old urn that had been left there. The rest of the terrace had been hand-weeded religiously clean to show off the grand house.

PLANTS ALONG THE PATH ⋘ The miniature trumpets of jonquils, pulmonaria's leaf spots, poppies' silky petals, the plum red undersides of begonia leaves—these details deserve places right alongside the path; the cosmos can go way to the back, unless you want to touch them as you walk by. If you want people to look down plants' throats—the flowers of orchids, mimulus, and foxgloves, for example, are much more delightful inside than out—raise the plants closer to eye level in a container. Place the container at the entrance to a path, at the intersection of two paths, or alongside a seat at the path's destination.

Showy roses or plants with striking forms or foliage, like yuccas, ornamental grasses, euphorbias, and topiary make good path turners, because they catch the eye from a distance and beckon you to see where the path goes next. Hide the next stretch of path with a twiggy shrub.

Hedges on either side of a path generate a lovely feeling of enclosure. As you walk along a clipped yew walk in an English garden on a summer morning, it's still and warm out of the wind, a place to watch a panel of sky and the yellow light on the dark hedge tops before emerging into the gardens with their misty pastel flowers and views of damp hayfields. Consider a hedge or thicket along a path to block an undesirable view, or to withhold a beautiful view until the point on the path where it will be seen at its best.

An umbrella-shaped tree alongside an exposed path provides shade and a natural place for a seat to watch the silhouette of the canopy flicker across the floor. Several tall, slim trees—Italian cypresses, fastigiate hornbeams—make a dramatic vertical line on flat land and, if they're spaced equidistantly, a pleasant rhythmic sense as you walk by them. Fruit trees on either side of a path turn an allée into an orchard; train the branches over a series of arches, and the fruit will hang through the tunnel over your head. Even in a small garden with room for only one tree, it's possible to choreograph a change of mood by running the path from sunlight into shade and then out again. Choose a medium- or small-sized tree for a garden path, so the branches arch over it and frame a garden view, and the flowers are low enough to see and smell. Avoid trees that drop honeydew or messy fruit that may stain the path or make it slippery. A tree with exfoliating or mottled bark should be close enough to touch.

Pathside plants must all merit the attention they'll get. Select the very best plants, with special flowers or special foliage and reputations for being resilient to unsightly pests and diseases; set up contrasts in texture, and decide from the start whether the colors will be harmonious or exhilarating. Consider how long the plants will flower, how they will look after they flower. Plan something for winter: berries, rosehips, crocuses, grasses to snap and stoop under the weight of snow, yew topiary to hold a geometric line of crunchy white hoarfrost on black green foliage, or deciduous shrubs to catch a headful of raindrops after a storm and burst into flower before spring.

When the path first goes in, its shape will stand out against the garden like a clear-cut on a hillside. The temptation is to disguise the hard edges with colorful plants that grow as fast as possible. Before you do that, first put in the permanent plants at the proper intervals and set back appropriately from the path. Then, if your imagination isn't strong enough to picture the eventual scene while you wait for the plants to grow, go ahead and fit quick-blooming annuals between the permanent plants, or better still, set out a line of showy plants in pots on the path. But don't neglect the permanent plants.

PATH EDGINGS ⪜⪜ Some paths need edgings to keep the base materials securely in place; gravel paths bordering vegetable or flower gardens need edgings to help prevent the gravel from traveling into the garden, which it invariably does when someone shuffles just once or the wheelbarrow plows up a spray. Aside from that, edgings are pure style.

In a formal garden where the gardener must not let down the grandeur of the house, brick paths are edged with a different, just as formal, pattern of the same brick. You can let the formality of brick unravel into mischief by allowing dirt from the bank to spill right over it in places or decorating it with bowls of marbles. At the late Ganna Walska's garden at Lotusland, in California, chunks of blue-green slag glass (waste from the manufacture of Coca-Cola bottles) line the bark paths and glow in sequence every time light passes across the woodland floor.

A simple gravel path can be dressed up with an edging of small boulders or a stretch of flowers arching over it. If the path runs through a garden of perennials, repeat clumps of each flower periodically along the path to set up a pleasing rhythm. For drama, flank both edges with the same plant and consider multiple edgings: a wooden strip, a low hedge, a line of cascading roses flanked by a trellis, or a colonnade of trees, all positioned parallel to the line of the path.

A HIERARCHY OF PATHS ≈≈≈ Not all paths are equal. The
paths that lead to utility areas need to look less inviting than the main path to the arbor and the ocean view, or the garden will seem chaotic and visitors will go nosing around the wrong corners. Even in a small garden, there's usually need for more than one path. The hierarchy is best planned on paper.

Draw out in any rough way the shape of the garden and the traffic routes around it. Consider who travels where and why. In one color outline the path that leads to the best feature of the garden. This will be your most lavishly announced path, the most generously detailed or planted path, and probably the broadest path. In a second color mark any subsidiary paths, ones leading to other pleasant destinations in the garden; these probably lead off from the main path and will be narrower or less lavish looking than the main path. In a third color mark the paths that are purely functional—they'll get you safely and quickly from the kitchen to the garbage area after dark or from the flower beds to the compost heap with an overladen wheelbarrow, or they'll get the kids from the den to the pool without running across the kitchen patio.

Edit the plan carefully. If the garden looks like a rabbit warren of paths, think about giving one path two purposes. The main path to the arbor may also be the path to the toolshed if, when it reaches the arbor, it turns to a dirt track that slips off behind a screen. Alternatively the toolshed can be the destination of the path, if you have a rack of polished tools, a vine tumbling over the old roof, and a place to sit with a view back over the garden.

In your mind's eye, position yourself at each house exit and examine the path logic from there. If three paths lead off from the back door, to avoid a confusing traffic junction, consider laying a terrace, playing up the main path off of it, and downplaying, even hiding, the other exits.

The paths that are entirely functional should lead as directly as possible from point A to point B, or people will forge a shortcut. They should be as wide as they need to be—3 feet wide for a wheelbarrow or a trash can—and comfortable underfoot. The material should be functional too. A stepping-stone path may be too uneven for a person carrying a garbage can at night. Children running to and from a pool will not like sharp gravel or hot tiles.

Although you won't want to advertise the route to the garbage area with a grand entrance to it or an eye-catching shrub where it turns a corner, you can choose materials that are both functional and pleasing. Once it's out of the public eye, you can decorate the path just as you please, widen it into an area for propagating vegetable plants, make it a place of your own.

Unless they lead to a utility area, paths down the side of the house may be rarely used. Concrete pavers set in a low-maintenance ground cover like mondo grass will do fine for the occasional traffic, but if windows face onto this area, put a lot of style into the planting. A dining room that gives on to a grove of three blood-red small maples, instead of a shared fence and the neighbor's dining room, may draw people out and around the house for a closer look.

ENTRANCE PATHS ≈≈≈ On the strip from the street to the front door, there's an opportunity to make a very favorable impression. A well-announced wide path that runs directly to the door, safe from cluttering pots and slippery moss, allows people to arrive with their poise intact.

At Susan Van Atta's home on a narrow road in the hills, it's clear where the entrance is, even on a dark night. From the edge of the asphalt, a bright white concrete path guides you through the tall pineapple guava hedge to the front door. It's a streak of 3-foot concrete squares laid end to end. You could be carrying armfuls of packages and not be able to see your feet, but there are no plants so close that you'd damage them or tip them over and no uneven surfaces underfoot to trip on. The plants are dramatic (see page 102) but all low-maintenance perennials and trees, so the entrance always looks well-maintained, welcoming, and elegant.

In an effort to put a front garden to use, it's tempting to weave the entrance path through it. But arriving then becomes a long journey through a collection of annuals and perennials or even waterfalls. Dogs and mail deliverers will push through a gap in the planting to find the quickest route to the door, and guests carrying ice chests and trays of watermelon may guiltily follow their example. If the front garden is the only space available to grow flowers and you know you can maintain them to a level of excellence year-round, put them off to one side of a direct route from the point of arrival to the front door. From that path, by all means run a small path in among the flowers for guests to explore if they wish.

Kent Gullickson's entrance path is indirect by necessity; it zigzags up a steep urban frontage between towering retaining walls. You're likely to have to park a half block away, but the booming sweet scent of angel's trumpet guides you to the house. The tree is planted up in the garden, but its branches arch over the walls, shaking shadows of the trumpets all over their surfaces. At the entrance to the concrete steps, spikes of a purple phormium in a pot also cast their shadows on the wall. The perfume is heavy as you step up to the first landing, where a pot of dramatic cacti stops you in your tracks for a moment. At the second landing, there's a sound of chuckling water coming from the direction in which you're headed and a snapping plastic iguana on the steps to distract you from the effort of climbing. At the top of the next flight of steps, through the dangling apricot trumpets, you arrive at the house, in the shade of a rice paper plant, which catches the night light of the street in the gray felty undersides of its giant leaves. On the flat now, passing fragrant white roses and the bamboo spout tipping water into a bowl of duckweed, you arrive at the porch rejuvenated by the climb, a world away from the street below.

MATERIALS ≈≈≈ There's an emporium of materials available for paving—everything from stones dug up in the excavations next door to tiny squares of tumbled Italian marble available from a specialist's catalog. Each material has its own sound and feel when walked on, gathers raindrops or absorbs them, turns dark in rain or pale over time, collects heat or stays cool, chips and gathers moss or remains straight edged, shiny, and sophisticated for all time. Touch and tap a wide range of materials and visualize them in your garden. How will they look on that scale, will they wear well in the traffic in that part of the garden, will they make the nice soft foil to your bright flower plantings, or are you perhaps looking for something with a bold texture or pattern for a path between plain hedges?

To make a garden room a seamless extension of the indoor living space, consider running the indoor flooring materials—tile, terra-cotta, or wood—straight over the threshold. To anchor a new house or extension to its site, use the same material in the paths that was used in the architecture, or a similar one; the two will blend and make one calm scene. Local stones and gravels

always look more natural than imported materials; the color will match exactly the ridges on the nearby hillsides or the dried-up streambeds, and the house and garden will seem to belong in their environment. For an exhilarating, loud effect, of course, avoid the native materials and go for an obviously manufactured or foreign product in non-natural colors. Color the cement, stud it with orange marbles, and don't undermine the effect with timid naturalistic planting.

The patterns and texture of paving also affect the mood of a garden. Brick laid lengthwise down the path will quicken your pace; a complex or horizontal pattern will slow you down. Narrow joints between cut stones make for a more elegant surface than broad joints, where daisies will seed. Even the joints in concrete establish a certain pattern and rhythm. Materials with the least amount of pattern or texture will most prettily show the shadow of a tree or a summer cloud.

Too much of anything becomes monotonous, so change the paving material or pattern to mark a shift from one area of the garden to another. A rough fieldstone path might change to formal cut stone, for example, as it passes under an arch from a side garden into the main garden. A brick path might change to stone if it widens into a terrace, because the small units of brick can look fussy in a large area. Even if you're looking at the floor, you see that the mood of the garden has changed, and your pace changes. Two or three different types of paving in a garden, even a small garden, liven it up.

Mark the intersections of paths and path destinations with a more fanciful or elegant paving pattern or by introducing a new material—handcarved stones, a few tiles, a brick circle—or an ornament, such as a simple water bowl. If you're using gravel or any other loose material, lay an apron of stone or brick or concrete at the house door and place a stiff doormat on top, to help keep the path material out of the house.

Avoid any material unsuitable for your climate. Ask specifically how each material will weather through your summers and winters. Certain bricks and terra-cotta tiles will crumble in frost, for example. Don't be miserable if you can't afford the most expensive stone in the catalogs. The least expensive materials usually look the most natural and harmonious. And, as the following chapters show, you can always dress them up cheaply by planting in the path or making fanciful edgings.

BUILDING PATHS

One Saturday starts with planning—choosing a path, checking through the design chapter and this practical chapter—then out to shop at a builders' supply yard to select materials. Put on sturdy boots and gloves so that you can scramble over piles of craggy rocks to find the ones with thick green moss or orange lichen, shovel up bagfuls of sharp mountain-gray gravel, soft buff sand, and shaggy bark that smells of forest, pick up and compare the sharp dark red brick with the mellow yellow brick, or sort through snapped pink and blue flagstones quarried in distant states and smooth river pebbles still water stained.

Another Saturday it's up early, in favorite old clothes and the gloves and the boots, for a day outdoors away from the phone. The work starts out warm and energetic, clearing and digging and hauling the materials into place. Then it's detail work, a quiet concentration to lay the brick pattern neatly to the edges or wet and roll the gravel so it crowns at the center. At the end of the day, evening light falls gold across the new brick or casts long shadows of young catmint plants across the new gravel.

Building a path is fun. Take it slowly; enjoy getting everything lined up right, before you start.

TOOLS ⇝⇝⇝ Marking out the path with neon-pink twine and corner pegs has a tickling satisfaction to it compared with dragging a thick hose about and trying to make it lie straight. There's no substitute for a straight-edged spade in making a clean perpendicular trench; any other kind leaves irritating ridges. A 6-foot piece of two-by-four, absolutely straight, will make leveling over a large area simple; just place the level on top of it. Or better still, buy a 6-foot level.

Start out with thick comfortable gloves if you're handling pavers or stones or brick. And a heavy-duty wheelbarrow that you can push around and empty easily. Wheel out all the tools you'll need, and spend a few moments visualizing how you'll complete each step in the recipe, where in the garden you'll spread the precious topsoil you remove, how you'll move the materials into position, the best time to take a break.

Building the base carefully is critical. The solid feel that great paths have, even in wet weather, results from a careful packing down of the base. If you're making a short run of path, invest in a hand-held tamping device, a heavy metal plate on a long handle, so you can get the base firm. If you're building a long run of path, rent a water-fillable drum roller or a plate vibrator. The work of building paths spins along nicely with good tools, leaving you to muse on your progress and dream of everything finished and grown in.

CLEARING AND LEVELING THE GROUND ⇜⇜ For an
easy life, avoid trying to lay a path over boggy ground (see Drainage, page 28) or aggressive roots. Some tree roots, blackberry roots, and bamboo roots will crack concrete. They'll make a hill out of mortared brick, and reclaim a path of gravel or bark in the first year. Check a plant encyclopedia if you're in any doubt, and avoid paving close to anything described as having aggressive or invasive roots. If you're paving close to any kind of tree, you can expect some heaving eventually. Gravel is a good choice in such a situation. The odd root can push through the surface without causing damage, and once it's clearly visible, so people won't trip, it makes a beautiful detail to the path.

Stepping-stones, bark, gravel, and grass flow beautifully over contoured land; the ground can tip and rise gently and the path will emphasize the natural lines. Unless you want a flat, uniform, formal look, you need grade only to the extent of filling potholes and leveling bumps.

Formal paths of brick, cut stone, and concrete pavers laid edge to edge don't work well on undulating land; the pattern and rhythm go out of kilter. Move soil about as necessary to make the path area flat, tamping it down firmly before you start making the path, and checking the grade carefully with a level atop a long piece of two-by-four. If necessary, grade the area beyond the path to prevent runoff from a slope flooding onto the path.

Clear the path area of weeds, paying particular attention to crabgrass, couch grass, Bermuda grass, bindweed, oxalis, and any other virulent perennial weed. A layer of landscape cloth between the path base and the path surface should block most weeds (but ensure that it's a superporous material so that water will drain quickly through it). If you're laying stepping-stones or loose materials straight over dirt, settle the weed problem before you start construction. Weed the ground, then water it to encourage weed seeds to sprout; reweed and water; wait a month, and weed the path area again. Once the path is laid, if weeds appear, clear them quickly; don't give them a chance to flower and reseed themselves.

MARKING OUT THE PATH PERIMETER ⋙ Before

you mark out the path is the moment to check that there's no nagging voice in your head warning that this path won't work out as well as you hope. Is it truly wide enough to take the catmint that will sprawl over the edges and still allow two people to amble along without wet ankles after rain? Does the path lead somewhere worth heading out to across the garden? Is there a plan for widening the path at the destination, making it interesting along the way? If doubts surface, dip into the chapter "Designing Paths," and review your plan.

An inexpensive mason's line, or twine, and stakes are the simplest tools for marking out the path boundaries. Rake the area level, then lay out the line. For straight paths made of brick, cut stone, or concrete pavers laid end to end, the path edges must be absolutely parallel for the pattern to work; check the width of the path at regular intervals. Mark out any setbacks off the path for a bench or a viewing point; be sure to allow a generous space for these and also for the destination of the path.

Curved paths are often marked out with a hose, but hoses snake easily and the resultant curves are too tight and fiddly to look natural in the garden. Use a hose if you like, but don't let its flexes guide your path shape. The same problem can occur if you use construction chalk; it's easy to sprinkle it in finicky unnatural lines. Unless you're jagging an informal path around a natural obstacle, such as a rock, a tree, or a thick clump of tall perennials, stick to bold curves, and draw them out in the ground as arcs of a circle. Stake the spindle of twine at the center of a circle (the radius might be the width or twice the width of the path), attach a marking stick to the end of the line, and draw an arc; move the center of the circle and adjust the length of the line to get the curve right. Once you've got it right, place pegs along the mark, in case it gets scuffed as you work.

Stepping-stone paths can be marked out in two ways. Either walk as nonchalantly as you can down the route in large boots on wet ground so you can see the natural positions for the stones, allowing yourself to step widely around a bush, detour toward a view, follow the line of the house, whatever seems most natural. Or, plan the rhythm of the stones on paper, perhaps referring to a Japanese tea ceremony guidebook—Japanese gardeners have developed many different ways of arranging stepping-stones to create a pleasing visual rhythm as guests approach the tea ceremony room. Whichever method you choose, place a large stone at the first step, at the destination, and at any intersections of paths along the way.

DRAINAGE ≋≋≋ A well-laid path on a porous base sheds water quickly: moisture flows down through the sand layer, through the porous landscape cloth, into the gravel or crushed rock, and from there into the soil. If the underlying soil has severe drainage problems, however, in heavy rains water will pool up through the layers of the path base and flood the surface. It's a simple task to check the likelihood of such flooding: Before you excavate the path, dig a hole roughly 12 inches around and 12 inches deep and fill it with water. Let it drain and then refill it. If it fails to drain the second time within twelve hours, you have poor drainage. In all but the most serious cases, you may solve this problem by using the deepest foundation recommended in the path instructions (see page 112 for calculating amounts of extra material), but if you have any concerns, consult a landscape architect or an experienced contractor who knows the soils in your area.

In rainy climates and formal situations, consider laying the path an inch above the surrounding soil level, so dirt doesn't wash onto it during a downpour. In areas of heavy rains, be particularly careful to contain the path within firm edgings so that the base materials do not wash out from underneath the surface. Paths close to the house need to slope just a little (3 inches over 8 yards) away from the house foundations. Allow room for metal flashing if you're laying a solid path material, like concrete, right up to the house wall. Laying the center of the path an inch higher than the edges will help ensure that water flows off to the sides instead of pooling in the center. In a path made of loose materials, like decomposed granite, the slightly raised, or crowned, center is a nice detail. Stepping-stones with concave surfaces will collect puddles; they will be too slippery for heavily used areas, especially in winter when the puddles may turn to ice, but can provide an interesting texture for a side path.

If your garden soil is clayey or gets soggy after rain, paths that are often laid without a deep foundation, such as stepping-stones or bark, will stay firmer and drier if you lay a base of gravel or crushed rock beneath them.

A PROPER BASE ⪢⪢ Paths can be laid in three ways: straight onto dirt, onto a layer of sand, or onto a deep foundation that includes crushed rock or gravel. (Always use angular, mechanically crushed gravel or rock for a path foundation, never the round, water-washed stone, such as pea gravel, which scatters instead of packing down tight.) The simplest method, of course, is to lay a path directly onto the dirt, saving yourself the trouble of digging a deep foundation trench and hauling in heavy loads of rock and sand. But a deep foundation has advantages too: Water drains quickly from a path built on a deep foundation, so you may prevent flooding and ice from closing the path. A deep foundation also greatly helps a path stay level; any movement in the underlying soil, due to hard ground frosts in winter or cracking in dry summers, is absorbed in the base materials, so the surface doesn't buckle or slip. A path laid on a deep base feels solid underfoot; gravels and other loose materials won't scatter so readily if rolled into packed sand on packed gravel or crushed rock. Brick and stone will last longer on a deep base and be less prone to tilting and cracking. In an entrance or a main artery through the garden, the stable surface provided by a deep base means a safer path.

Do the drainage test described on page xx if you're unsure of your soil's drainage. If the soil drains well, next consider the soil stability. In Florida, the South, and southern and coastal California, soils are generally stable, and paths do not require the deep base needed for paths laid in the northern half of the country, where the ground freezes hard in winter. With these two pieces of information—drainage and stability—in hand, you can follow the recommendations given for each path, at the beginning of the How to Do It section. If your climate and soil fall between the options given, you might decide to skimp a little on the deep base materials, especially if you're laying an informal path, in a situation where it really isn't critical that the path be even.

None of the recipes in this book includes a base of concrete. Stretches of

concrete are somewhat difficult for an inexperienced person to get right the first time; concrete is a heavy material, and breaking it up and re-laying it is a nightmarish prospect. Although a concrete base and mortared paving units might seem to be the surest way to make a path firm, concrete will crack and heave eventually, and then the job of resettling the surface is extremely difficult. Better to lay the path on a deep foundation of rock and sand, mortar the edges if necessary, and, when the surface buckles, simply pick up the units and respread the sand.

PATHS ON SLOPES Paths that slope about 1 foot over 10 feet feel comfortable for most people; a drop any steeper than that may be leveled out in two ways. The more expensive option, and the more visually dramatic, is to terrace the ground flat behind retaining walls and have the path descend flights of stairs from terrace to terrace. Outdoor staircases, like outdoor fireplaces, are exciting garden features. They can be made to spiral or zigzag from landing to landing or descend headlong down the grade in grand formal straightness. The inexpensive option is to weave the path back and forth across the slope, taking some of the drama out of the drop but stretching out the experience of the garden.

Gravels are the most natural looking and perhaps safest materials for sloping paths. Brick and cut stone and grass become slippery after rain. Lay a sloping path on a deep foundation so it drains quickly. In areas of heavy rainfall, use the largest grade of crushed rock in the foundation, because it will wash away less easily. Always work from the bottom of the slope up; that way, you can pack the materials more firmly against each other. Be sure to grade the bank so that soil doesn't wash or slide onto the path; if necessary, retain it with sturdy timber and stakes.

On a steep stretch, dig an occasional stepping-stone or railroad tie step into the path. On a very steep stretch, consider making a staircase of overlapping stepping-stones; work from the base of the slope uphill, digging each stone firmly back into the grade onto a deep foundation of sand, or sand and crushed rock, and mortaring the stones together where they touch. For stability and safety, choose broad timber or large, thick stones with rough surfaces but no indentations to collect ice. And be sure the steps stand out visually from the rest of the path, so no one trips; the more occasional the step, the better advertised it should be. A single step on a slope should be loudly announced.

Where a path cuts across a steep slope, dig a drainage ditch alongside the path, on the bank side, and lay 4-inch drainage pipes crosswise periodically in the path foundation to move the water from the ditch under the path and down the slope. Alternatively, in areas where it's not inconvenient if the path gets waterlogged now and then, and impassable without boots, consider a bark or sawdust path. When it's swept downslope in the rain, accept it as mulch for the plantings, and order in new material at the start of the dry season.

CLIMATE AND PAVING CHOICE ⪮⪮⪮ Paving materials have

different characteristics: some are frost-proof, some waterproof; some absorb heat, some reflect it and cause dazzle; some get slippery either because the surface is so sleek, or because they are pocked and collect water and ice. Run through the changes in your climate from season to season, and think about who will be walking the paths and what they will be wearing on their feet.

In harsh winter climates where the ground freezes, terra-cotta and soft brick will crumble, concrete may crack, slate will be slippery, brick and light-colored (but not white) gravel will look warm. Most paths need a deep foundation to stay firm underfoot after heavy storms. Grass paths become unwalkable for months unless there's a stepping-stone bridge.

In hot summer areas, grass is cool and soft underfoot, and it will grow well as long as the area receives enough moisture and sunlight; choose a grass mixture suitable for your region, so the path doesn't go bare and need repeated reseeding. Light-colored gravel may be too dazzling in the bright sun, tile too hot.

EDGINGS ⪮⪮⪮ Practically speaking, an edging is a device for containment. It helps keep soil or lawn grasses or ground covers from creeping onto the path and the paving material from sliding into the flower beds. In the most informal situations, an edging is unnecessary: perhaps it really doesn't matter if gravel crosses into the beds, forget-me-nots germinate in the path, and a brick on the path edge tilts on the rare occasion when someone steps there. In other situations, an edging is important for safety, or to increase the path's durability, or to lend a lively sense of detail and style.

Benderboard costs the least and installs fairly easily, though you need to tack two layers together to get a sturdy edge. It sits up tight against the paving, secured by stakes driven into the soil on the outside edge. For gentle curves, soak the boards overnight in water, so they bend more easily. For tight curves, use plastic or aluminum edgings. Most woods rot quickly in damp soils, so for the stakes and boards always choose heartwood cedar or redwood, or pressure-treated woods (handle these environmentally unfriendly products with gloves and a mask, and use them only where their ugly and slow-to-fade greenish color won't show).

Wood edgings of two-by-fours—or two-by-sixes for heavily trafficked paths with a deep base—are relatively inexpensive and easy to install. At a corner, nail the two pieces of edging together first to make an L, then place them into the trench, and nail them to the stakes. For curves, use wooden benderboard: nail one piece to a set of stakes that defines the curve, and build up the desired thickness with additional lengths of benderboard, nailing them together and to the stakes.

Bricks or four-by-fours make a convenient level edge for a path that borders a lawn. Position the wood or brick flush with the lawn (where the grasses meet the soil surface), so that you can run the mower with one wheel on the edging and make a good, clean cut.

Preformed plastic edgings work well with brick paths and concrete pavers. A stiff band sits against the bricks or pavers and keeps them in line; at the base of the band, below soil level, are plastic loops for spikes that you hammer into the ground.

River stones and boulders look most natural if you bury the bottom one-third of them. Left on the surface, they look like a necklace. Flagstones at a path edge may tip and crack if they get a lot of traffic; to prevent that, set the stones at the path edge in a 1-inch bed of mortar and contain the base below the mortar with a strong edging. Check the points where people will walk over the path edge, where the path meets the doors or the patio; secure these edges well, resting them in a base of mortar if there's any concern about safety.

BUYING AND TRANSPORTING PAVING MATERIALS

⋙ Garden centers and nurseries usually have only the smallest choice of paving materials, if any. Check the Yellow Pages under these categories: Brick, Building Materials, Cement, Concrete Products, Landscaping Equipment and Supplies, Lumber–Retail, Lumber–Used, Quarries, Rock, Sawdust, Sod, Stone–Natural, Tile. Contractors and landscape architects buy from these sources. You'll discover everything from heavy railroad ties oozing tar bubbles to delicate little outdoor carpet squares of marble mosaic.

Once you've found the path surface material, the foundation materials, and the edging material, calculate how much you need of each (the recipes usually indicate quantities per yard length of path; if you're adapting a recipe, see "Calculating Quantities of Materials" on page 112 to work out what you'll need). Purchase a little extra, in case you need to do repair work in the future. It's a nuisance to try to match brick or stone when the original batch has sold.

Don't skimp on quality. It will be a dreadful headache to lift and discard broken stone or bricks and start over with new material because the original batch was too thin or soft. Avoid buying small stepping-stones; they won't look graceful or generous. For wood edgings, always buy heartwood cedar or redwood or lumber that has been treated, because other lumber won't last and it's a hard job replacing edgings. Question a sod dealer about the freshness of the sod; it needs to have been freshly harvested from the sod farm, especially in hot weather. Buy direct if you can.

Place the order all at once and consider having the company deliver it. Many paving materials are heavy; if you plan on picking them up yourself, first calculate the weight roughly with the supplier and check that your vehicle is rated for that load weight.

Decide on a delivery site as close as possible to the new path. If gravel or sand is being dumped loose, spread a tarp across the ground, so you won't be forever trying to pick up the last bits of stone out of the grass. Ask whether the delivery person can position individual large stones in their final places. If the answer is yes, dig the holes right away; it will save you the time-consuming work of sliding heavy boulders over log rollers or dragging them with chains or levering them into and out of a wheelbarrow. Boulders with patches of moss or lichen deserve special treatment to keep them from getting scratched and scraped bare; drag them into place on old pieces of carpet.

BUYING PLANTS FOR PATH EDGES ⋙ Newly laid paths can look stark until plants begin to grow and soften the edges. Plants will grow quickly if they were well taken care of in the nursery and you plant them properly. Choose strong, healthy plants, with no evidence of pests or disease and no anemic-looking leaves or roots tangling out of the bottom of the pot. Take the ones with the most shoots from the base, or the most branches;

leave the thin, spindly samples, even if they are in pretty flower. For the fastest cover, perhaps choose the largest plants, though sometimes it's not worth the extra expense, because smaller plants will take off faster when planted and grow thicker than ones already large when purchased. If there's a choice of sizes, ask a nursery person what to expect in terms of growth.

Before you leave the nursery, check the plant label for special soil requirements. If the plant needs rich soil, and you haven't recently dug in compost or manure, pick some up from the nursery and dig it in before you plant. If the label mentions well-drained soil and you know your ground is often soggy or clayey, choose a different plant. Ask the nursery person to recommend a substitute; consider the flower color, the plant height and spread, and the foliage color and texture. Good nurseries will be delighted to provide suggestions.

PLANTING THE PLANTS ⋞⋞⋞ Plant as soon as you can. Unless you're a skilled gardener, some will decline rapidly if left around in their pots for a month. Dig a hole as deep as the pot and a little wider. The bottom of the hole is best left flat for perennials; for shrubs and trees, dig a trench around the perimeter of the bottom, leaving a mound in the center for the plant to sit on.

Water the plant in its pot, then gently tip it out into your hands. Plants in cell-packs can be pushed up and out by poking your thumb underneath each cell. If a plant doesn't slip easily out of a plastic pot, slide a knife between the soil and the pot, tip the pot onto its side and tap the base of the pot, holding the plant by its stem. Trees sometimes won't slip out of heavy plastic or metal pots without cutting the pot—make a slit from the rim to the base. Be a little careful with the knife, so as not to cut through big roots, but don't worry about slicing into a thick mat of small roots.

Take a hard look at the plant's rootball. Many plants have been in nurseries too long and the roots have had nowhere to grow but around and around into a dense mat. Rootballs like these slide out of the pot in one solid mass; if there was growing room to spare, loose soil will tumble from the pot. To help plants with matted rootballs get off to a good start, do some surgery. With your thumb or a sharp knife, score into the rootball, from top to bottom, several places around the circumference. With your fingers, pry the roots loose, breaking the small, thin roots as you need to, but being careful not to snap thick roots. Freed from the tight tangle, the roots will now quickly grow out into fresh soil. Prune off any rotten or diseased roots.

Place the plant in the planting hole. The top of the rootball must be slightly above the soil surface, at least an inch above for trees. Planted too deeply, the stem is likely to rot. If a tree needs staking, drive the stake deep into the ground on one side of the rootball. Fill in around the rootball with the soil you removed to dig the hole, packing it firmly, and lifting the plant if necessary to keep it above the soil level. Handle the plant always by the main stem.

Press the soil firmly around the plant. The soil must make contact with the roots; if there are air pockets around the roots, they'll die. Make a watering moat, and water the plant generously. Raise the plant and refirm it if necessary. If you're staking a tree, loop the tie from stake to tree loosely.

Until the plant starts to produce new growth and is obviously established, water regularly. The soil should never dry out 2 inches below the surface. Once they are established, drought-tolerant plants will need less frequent watering. Keep watering other plants regularly.

PATH MAINTENANCE ⇔⇔⇔ Cut stone laid end to end, on a firm

deep base, with a strong edging, needs only an occasional hosing or sweeping. Grass, by contrast, needs constant care unless the mix is a native one or very carefully matched to your climate. Gravel needs regular raking and weeding, and a light replenishing every year or two (a layer of landscape cloth below the gravel will reduce the need for weeding). Tightly laid brick will need less weeding than brick spaced widely so that moss and grass can grow in the cracks. Mortared joints will not need weeding if you check and renew the mortar periodically, but the path becomes much harder to re-lay if it starts to heave. Stepping-stones are low in maintenance, as long as they are firmly laid and the surrounding plants are not invasive.

In wet or snowy weather, sprinkle sand over stone and brick and smooth-finished concrete to increase traction and prevent accidents. For safety reasons, keep all paths clear of rotting debris, which can be very slippery.

Before you choose a path recipe, check the maintenance information in the recipe list. Decide how you'd get the maintenance done, how long it might take. Perhaps it wouldn't be a nuisance—there's something satisfying about revisiting a path you've built, wheeling out the familiar tools, donning your favorite gardening gloves, working your way yard by yard down the path, pulling out the weeds before they reseed, perhaps pushing in miniature bulbs, setting it up neatly for another year.

BRICK

Winston Churchill built the gardens at Chartwell with brick. Standard and bush roses in all colors stand out cleanly against the high brick walls and arch over the straight brick paths. In the rain, the brick is as dark a red as a Mister Lincoln; on dry, warm evenings, it's as pale and soft as old pink moss roses. It's not an inexpensive hobby, but laying brick in the fresh air, resting when you want to, is simple and gratifying. Later, when you're catching up with the inevitable weeding of the joints, you get to appreciate the lovely way brick ages.

Brick paths in tight herringbone or basketweave patterns, bordered with neat soldier panels of bricks turned on edge, proclaim elegance, expense, tradition. But they can be loosened up in a number of ways to suit a more informal situation. Make a patchwork path of brick and stone and tile, or let the edges wiggle and leave 1-inch gaps between the bricks so that flowers and moss can really take hold.

Brick has an earthy-red, natural color to it that warms up a chill, damp garden; in cold climates, it's more welcoming than slate or granite. New brick is a little flat and hard until it starts to weather. Help the mosses and stains along by dousing the brick in a yogurt or manure solution. Test a few different colors of brick by borrowing samples from the supplier and leaving them about in the garden for a few days. See that the color goes with the house and any walls or fences nearby.

Don't be tempted to use old bricks from interior house walls. They are easier to find than old bricks fired especially for outdoor use, but they're soft; they'll flake and chip quickly, and turn to brick dust after a hard frost. In damp areas of the garden, search for bricks with a textured surface; they'll be less slippery after rain.

Working a pattern up to the edging sometimes requires a half brick. Put on safety glasses to protect your eyes, and use a brick set (a 3½-inch cold chisel). Put the brick on the soil, place the brick set halfway along the brick, and hammer it gently, scoring a line in the brick. Score all four sides of the brick, position the brick set on a score line, and break the brick by delivering a sharp blow with the hammer.

FORMAL BASKETWEAVE AND TULIPS

Dampness settles here at the edge of the woodland, sustaining lichen on the branches of the camperdown elms and moss in the walls of the outhouse. The building smells musty inside, fungal, and the hose faucet outside gets rusty. It would be a dank, dreary place if gray stone had been the choice instead of warm brick. In early spring, when the bare elms are shiny with fog, the brick contains pockets of dry, rosy lightness that are highlighted by the tulips' pale pink and apricot-yellow petals. Scarlet tulips make their way up later, to pick out the red in the brick and in the emerging bracts of the elms.

HOW TO DO IT ≈≈≈

This path is laid on a foundation of 4 inches of gravel, a layer of landscape cloth (optional), and 2 inches of sand; a firm, long-lasting base suitable for most situations. If your soil freezes hard or drains poorly, lay 4 inches of crushed rock (1½-inch), a layer of landscape cloth, 2 inches of gravel, and 2 inches of sand. The edges of this path are dry-mortared for stability. The base materials are contained by an invisible plastic edging.

Before you start, measure the dimensions of your bricks, to determine the size of the gap you should leave between them in the central panel of the path. Double the width of the brick and subtract that number from the length of the brick. For example, if your bricks are 3⅝ inches wide and 7⅝ inches long, the pattern will work smoothly if you leave ⅜-inch gaps. Choose bricks that will work with gaps no greater than ½ inch; smaller gaps make a more stable path.

Clear any weeds, and rake the ground level. Mark out the path perimeter with the twine and stakes; make it 5 feet wide.

Dig an 8-inch trench the length and width of the path; firm the bottom of the trench if you've disturbed the soil while digging. Spread 2 inches of gravel into the bottom of the trench. Moisten this layer, and pack down the surface with the tamper or roller. Lay the next 2 inches in the same way.

Across the top of the gravel, lay a sheet of porous landscape cloth (optional), to prevent weeds from growing up from the ground and sand from filtering down, over time, into the gravel.

Lay the plastic edging along the edges of the trench, with its stake holes on the outside. To check the path width between the edgings, lay 6 bricks lengthwise across the path, the outer two flush against the plastic edging and ⅜-inch joints (or whatever gap works with your bricks) between the rest. Adjust the edgings as necessary. Once the width is right, secure the edgings by hammering the stakes through the edging holes into the ground.

Spread 1 inch of sand over the gravel base. Dampen the sand and tamp it, level it by drawing the two-by-four across it, and tamp again. Check with the level that the sand bed is even.

Lay the sides of the path first. Working from a knee pad in the center of the path, lay bricks on edge, narrow sides up (as shown in the photograph), along the path edges, flush against the plastic edging. Insert the ¼-inch joint spacer against each laid brick before laying the next brick against it, to make the

Moderately inexpensive
Moderately difficult
Location: Sun or light shade

Tools
Measuring tape
Rake
Twine and stakes
Straight-edged spade, for digging
Shovel, for spreading materials
Hose
Hand-held tamper or water-fillable roller
Joint spacers: 8-inch piece of ¼-inch plywood, plus 8-inch piece of plywood the thickness of your brick joints (see text)
Hammer
Piece of straight two-by-four, 2½ feet long, for leveling sand
Level
Knee pad
Rubber mallet
Small hand broom
Rubber gloves
Container for mixing mortar
Planting trowel
Piece of plywood, for kneeling on bricks
Cloth, for wiping up mortar

Ingredients
Bricks, 65 per 1 yard of path
Gravel, sharp-edged, ⅜- or ¼-inch, 5½ cubic feet per 1 yard of path
Landscape cloth, 5 feet by length of path (optional)
Plastic preformed invisible edging for bricks, with stakes, length of perimeter
Builder's sand, 2¼ cubic feet per 1 yard of path
Cement, small bag
Apricot Beauty tulips, 12 per 1 yard of path
Terra-cotta 14-inch pots
Potting soil
Daydream tulips, 24 per pot

Maintenance
Water tulips, unless it rains, every 5 days from the time leaves emerge through flowering
When flowers fade, cut flower stalks but let leaves die back before trimming
Refill joints with sand as necessary

joints between bricks even. Place the bricks directly on top of the sand; don't wedge or push them in. Try to keep the sand bed level and undisturbed. Settle each brick as you lay it by tapping it with the mallet. With the level, check that it's flush with the other bricks; if necessary, lift the brick and spread a little more sand underneath it.

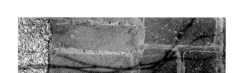

Before laying the center of the path, spread about 1 inch more sand over the sand bed, so that when you lay the bricks flat side up they'll be flush with the side bricks you've just laid on edge. Dampen the sand, tamp it, level it, and tamp again. Check with the level that the sand bed is even.

Lay the bricks in a single basketweave pattern, as shown in the photograph, using the spacer for your gap width at the joints and checking for evenness with the level. If you have difficulty keeping the pattern aligned, stretch twine across the path as a horizontal guide. Move the twine after every row of bricks.

As you finish 2 feet or so of path, fill the joints in the center of the path with sand. (Leave the joints on the sides of the path for later.) Spread the dry sand over the bricks and sweep it gently into the joints, to within ¼ inch of the path surface. When the last section of path is down, firm the soil against the outside of the plastic edgings.

Put on the rubber gloves to keep the cement off your skin. Mix the dry mortar—1 part cement with 4 parts sand. With the planting trowel, sift it carefully into the joints between the bricks on the sides of the path, just a little at a time, sweeping off any that spills onto the bricks, because it will stain. Tamp the dry mortar into the joints with the spacer, adding more mortar as necessary to bring it to within ¼ inch of the path surface. If you have to kneel on the path, put down a piece of plywood and kneel on that, so as not to move the bricks.

To finish the path, sprinkle it with a very fine spray from the hose, to settle the sand and mortar in the joints. Be careful not to splash the mortar mix onto the path surface. If any does escape, wipe it off immediately with the cloth. Don't walk on the mortared edgings for several days. Top up the sand in the other joints as necessary.

Plant the Apricot Beauty tulips in October (December in warm-winter climates), 6 inches deep and 6 inches apart, in two staggered rows. Fill the terracotta pots with potting soil; plant 24 Daydream tulips per pot. Water weekly until the rainy season starts.

QUICK BRICK CIRCLE

A craftsperson lays smooth, new bricks on a carefully excavated and packed base, filling the uniform ¼-inch joints with fine sand, not a single brick breaking the flat, red surface. A century later, time has made its own imprint. The bricks, grayer and softer now, fade into the plantings more; the textured surfaces harbor bubbles of spongy, apple-green moss; the edges have broken free in places; and the center of the path is dipping from so much wear.

This lovely degeneration of brick can be brought about quickly by skipping all the hard work usually employed to preserve brick. Lay a brick path directly onto dirt, and the bricks will start to shift and tilt from the moment they're down. Choose bricks already old, uneven, pocked, even cement-splashed, and pour a plain yogurt solution over them to get the algae and moss started. The path won't last long exactly as you've laid it, but you can always remove a few bricks one afternoon and straighten things out or march the whole thing off in a wheelbarrow to a new garden.

HOW TO DO IT ⟫⟫⟫ This path is laid directly on top of the soil without a foundation; it will shift and heave naturally. If your soil freezes hard or drains poorly, make a firm foundation: dig an 8-inch trench, and lay 4 inches of crushed rock (1½-inch), 2 inches of gravel, and 2 inches of sand.

Clear any weeds, and rake the ground level. Stand where the urn will be, and draw a circle in the dirt 3½ feet in radius (7 feet across), using the twine and two stakes. Place the concrete paver at the center of the circle, for the urn.

Lay the first ring of bricks end to end, flat sides up, following the line in the dirt. Adjust the gaps between them to close the circle, or use a half brick. (To cut a brick in half, see page 38.) Lay the next ring of bricks against the first ring, in a running bond pattern, as shown in the photograph. Keep the path surface level as best you can; it will settle irregularly.

Lay seven rings of brick to complete the circular path. Make an edging on each side of it by laying bricks narrow sides up and settling them into the dirt until they are about ½ inch above the path surface. Where the outer edge meets the straight path, bury the edging flush with the path.

Start the straight path with the middle row of bricks. Align it perfectly on the center of the circle; the eye can pick up even a small deviation, and this misalignment will be jarring. Lay three rows of brick on either side of the middle row, filling in with half bricks.

Shovel sand over the bricks, and brush it into the cracks. Brush off any excess. Water the path gently, to settle the sand; apply a second batch, and water gently.

Spread compost over the planting areas, to bring the soil level to within 1 inch of the path surface. Mix the compost into the soil.

Plant the Mexican daisies in the circle, 8 inches from the path edge. Plant the santolinas between the daisies and the urn. Place the urn on the paver, fill it with potting soil, and plant the morning glory. Plant the outer edges of the circle and path with catmint, 8 inches from the path, 2 feet apart.

Moderately inexpensive
Easy
Location: Sun

Tools

Rake
Measuring tape
Twine and stakes
Brick set or wide chisel
Hammer
Safety glasses and gloves
Shovel
Broom
Hose or watering can
Planting trowel

Ingredients

Urn, with drainage hole
1 concrete paver, or 4 bricks
Bricks, approx. 425 for circle, 35 per 1 yard
    of straight path (plus 10 per yard to
    edge straight path like circle)
Builder's sand, approx. 2 bags
Compost, approx. 3 bags
9 Mexican, or Santa Barbara, daisies
    (Erigeron karvinskianus)
6 santolinas (Santolina virens)
Potting soil, to fill urn
1 blue morning glory (Convolvulus
    sabatius)
21 catmint (Nepeta x faassenii) for circle,
    plus 3 per 1 yard of straight path

Maintenance

Water plants regularly until established,
    then less frequently
Fertilize plants with slow-release fertilizer
    in spring
Shear dead flower spikes if unsightly; may
    rebloom after shearing
Cut back plants to 6 inches in late fall, to
    regrow in spring
Resettle bricks that become a nuisance

CORRIDOR OF MIRRORS, FOUND OBJECTS

For a moment, in the shady corridor between the house and the garage, it looks as if there are windows that open onto a brightly lit garden, deep and pretty with flowers and ornaments. Three mirrors bounce sunlight and reflections all around the narrow space, catching and doubling the pink hydrangea heads, the upturned mannequin legs off to one side by the house gutter, and the bowls of marbles and rusty coils that edge the brick path.

The mirrors remind garden designer Sharon Osmond of a peephole at Sissinghurst gardens in England. Walking in the shade beside a tall yew hedge, you suddenly come upon a circular opening in the hedge that reveals a garden room furnished with sunlight and white roses.

HOW TO DO IT ≈≈≈ This path is laid on a foundation of 4 inches of gravel, a layer of landscape cloth (optional), and 2 inches of sand; a firm, long-lasting base suitable for most situations. If your soil freezes hard or drains poorly, lay 4 inches of crushed rock (1½-inch), a layer of landscape cloth, 2 inches of gravel, and 2 inches of sand. The path has no edging—plants and soil and found objects spill from the beds. The outside bricks may shift and tilt over time.

Before you start, measure the dimensions of your bricks, to determine the size of the gap you should leave between them so that the herringbone pattern works. Double the width of the brick and subtract that number from the length of the brick. For example, if your bricks are 3⅝ inches wide and 7⅝ inches long, the pattern will work smoothly if you leave ⅜-inch gaps. Sharon's bricks are large, and the gaps are wide.

Clear any weeds, and rake the ground level. Mark out the path perimeter with the twine and stakes; make it 3 feet wide.

Dig an 8-inch trench the length and width of the path. In dry climates, mound the soil into the flower beds on either side, to raise them above the path surface and better display the plants; in wet climates, carry the soil away so that it won't flood routinely over the path. Firm the bottom of the trench if you've disturbed the soil while digging. Spread 2 inches of gravel into the bottom of the trench. Moisten this layer, and pack down the surface with the tamper or roller. Lay the next 2 inches in the same way.

Across the top of the gravel, lay a sheet of porous landscape cloth (optional), to prevent weeds from growing up from the ground and sand from filtering down, over time, into the gravel.

To finish the foundation, spread 2 inches of sand. Dampen the sand, tamp it, and level it by pulling the two-by-four across it in a side-to-side sawing motion. Tamp one more time. Check that the sand bed is even by placing the level on the piece of two-by-four.

Working from a knee pad in the center of the path, lay the bricks in a herringbone pattern, as shown in the photograph. To start the pattern, lay one brick horizontally, a half brick next to it, then one brick vertically; repeat across the path width. (To cut a brick in half, see page 38.)

Place the bricks directly on top of the sand; don't wedge or push them in. Use the plywood joint spacer to set the gap between each brick. Try to keep

Moderately inexpensive
Moderately easy
Location: Shade

Tools
Measuring tape
Joint spacer: 8-inch piece of plywood the thickness of your brick joints (see text)
Rake
Twine and stakes
Straight-edged spade, for digging
Shovel, for spreading materials
Hose
Hand-held tamper or water-fillable roller
Piece of straight two-by-four, 2½ feet long, for leveling sand
Level
Knee pad
Brick set, or wide chisel, for cutting bricks
Safety glasses and gloves
Rubber mallet
Small hand broom
Plywood, for kneeling on bricks (optional)
Planting trowel

Ingredients
Gravel, sharp-edged, ⅝- or ¾-inch, 3¼ cubic feet per 1 yard of path
Landscape cloth, 3 feet by length of path (optional)
Builder's sand, 1¾ cubic feet per 1 yard of path
Bricks, 35 to 45 per 1 yard of path, depending on brick size (see text)
Mirrors, old framed ones or mirror panels
Found objects
Shade-loving fine-leaved vines, such as fiveleaf akebia (Akebia quinata), variegated or plain form
Shade-loving ground covers, such as bellflower (Campanula spp.)
Shade-loving bed plants, such as hydrangea, bamboo, lungwort (Pulmonaria spp.), pittosporum

Maintenance
Water plants regularly
Brush back soil spilling from beds
Refill joints with sand, as necessary
Resettle bricks at edges, as necessary

the sand level and undisturbed. Settle each brick as you lay it by tapping it with the mallet. With the level, check that it's flush with the other bricks; if necessary, lift the brick and spread a little more sand underneath it.

As you move down the path, try to keep the sand bed level. To fill dips, sprinkle extra sand on the bed and level it. If you have difficulty keeping the pattern aligned, stretch twine across the path as a horizontal guide. Move the line after every row or two of bricks.

As you finish every 2 feet or so of path, spread dry sand over the bricks and sweep it gently into the joints, to within ¼ inch of the path surface. If you have to kneel on the laid bricks, put down a piece of plywood and kneel on that, so as not to move the bricks. To finish the path, sprinkle it with a fine spray from the hose, to settle the sand in the joints. Top up the sand as necessary.

Hang the mirrors to pick up light and interesting reflections; keep them out of full sun, because they can be too dazzling. Set the found objects on the path edges. Plant the shade-loving plants on either side of the path: vines to frame the mirrors, creeping ground covers to sprawl onto the path, and, for the beds, a few plants with shiny or mottled or variegated or golden foliage, to mimic the effect of light.

SPRINGTIME PICTURE

Many elements in this picture, painted by artist and garden designer Keeyla Meadows, are the same sunny yellow: the flowers, parts of the fountain, and the tiles in the path. Placed against the flat hardscape yellow, the yellow columbines seem more transparent, the yellow tulips more curved, the shades of yellow in the narcissus bud more delicate.

Sunlight filters into the garden, casting shadows under leaves and between tiles, and shimmering light on the primroses and the ceramic flowers on the fountain. The light weaves the natural material and the art together into one picture, and the path leads you into it.

HOW TO DO IT ❧❧❧ This path is laid on a foundation of 2 inches of sand, a minimal base suitable only for freely draining soils that do not freeze hard in winter. If your soil freezes hard or drains poorly, lay 4 inches of crushed rock (1½-inch), 2 inches of gravel, and 2 inches of sand.

Instead of a Keeyla Meadows fountain as a focal point, you might choose a yellow pot on a pedestal or a yellow urn planted with yellow flowers. Take the tile with you when you shop, to match the yellows.

Clear any weeds, and rake the ground level. Mark out the path perimeter with the twine and stakes or construction chalk; make the path approximately 3½ feet wide and the area with tiles, where the path reaches the fountain, approximately 6 feet square. Keep the lines fluid, without sharp corners.

Dig a 4-inch trench the length and width of the path and tile area; spread the soil onto the flower beds, to raise them and better show off the plants.

Place the edging stones inside the trench, around the perimeter. Firm the bottom of the trench if you've disturbed the soil while digging. Spread 2 inches of sand into the trench, rake it, and compact it with the tamper or roller. Use the back of the trowel to pack the sand firmly around the edging stones. Dampen the sand and tamp it again. Check with a level that the sand bed is even.

Lay the area with the tiles first. Place the tiles in position. Align the tip of a yellow tile on the center of the fountain. Lay another tile alongside the first, tip to tip, then the next row of tiles to make the diamond checkerboard pattern, as shown in the photograph. (Next you'll lay out the bricks and stones, and then you'll put more sand under the tiles.)

Fill in between the tiles with sets of three bricks or a pair of stones, and fill around the path edges with combinations of brick pieces and

Moderately inexpensive
Moderately easy
Location: Sun or light shade

Tools
Rake
Measuring tape
Twine and stakes or construction chalk
Straight-edged spade, for digging
Shovel, for spreading sand
Hand-held tamper or water-fillable roller
Planting trowel
Hose
Level
Brick set, or wide chisel, for cutting brick
Safety glasses and gloves
Rubber mallet

Ingredients
Stones for edging, local, at least 8 inches
    thick, approx. 1½ wheelbarrowfuls for
    checkerboard area, ½ wheelbarrowful
    per 1 yard of path
Builder's sand, 1½ cubic feet per 1 yard of
    path, plus 5½ cubic feet for checker-
    board area
11 yellow tiles, frost-proof if necessary, at
    least 1 inch thick; 8 inches square will
    fit well with brick
Bricks, used, 50 for checkerboard area, 36
    per 1 yard of path
Stones for path, local, small, flat on one
    side, 5 to 8 per 1 yard of path
Small grasses, such as green and varie-
    gated forms of lily turf (Liriope spp.)
    and acorus
Yellow-flowered tulips, calceolarias,
    columbines (Aquilegia spp.), freesias,
    daffodils, primulas, corydalis

Maintenance
Water plants regularly
Resettle any bricks or stones that become
    a nuisance

stones. (To cut a brick, see page 38.) Lay the stones flat side up; bury them until the tops are level with the bricks.

As you lay the single tiles at the entrance to the checkerboard area, transition into a diagonal herringbone brick pattern for the rest of the path (as shown in the photograph). Substitute stones for bricks occasionally, and fill in any corners with stones.

Spread sand beneath the tiles, so they're flush with the bricks. Tap each tile with the mallet to settle it.

Plant the grasses to spill over the stones. Plant the yellow perennials, annuals, and bulbs in repeated clumps around the path and behind the fountain.

GRAVEL

Gravels make the loveliest sounds: decomposed granites, or small gravel chips with their dusty particles (fines) rolled in, emit soft thuds underfoot, like the sound of sand castles sliding out of sand buckets. Crushed gravels crunch as the sharp-angled chips grate against each other, a brief, crisp sound that stops as soon as the chips lock together. Round gravels, washed smooth by water, click and click and click, dragging your feet because instead of locking, they sink and roll.

Any kind of gravel runs beautifully under loose plantings of delicate flowers. Sooner or later, seeds will spill from a flower stalk tipping over the path edge and land in a pocket of mud in the gravel and germinate. As a few plants colonize the path and the gravel wears thin over the underlying rock, the lines between the path and the garden blur until the path disappears into an overgrown trail.

Here in a hillside garden of poppies and cacti, the show is different every spring. Some of the poppies bloom pale, some reddish, some pure gold. The variations in the silky petals are matched in the huge stones — chosen for their striations of blood-red, honey, and ochre — the spiky-sharp, red berberis branches, and the particles of decomposed granite in infinite gradations of gold and custard and wheat.

Gravel makes an altogether different, perfectly formal pathway if edged with something clipped and neat, like grass or a holly or boxwood hedge. In many old gardens, brick and stone lined the walks and terraces closest to the house, then gravel took over as the paths passed through arches into the vegetable garden or the woodland garden. The brick and stone were kinder to expensive leather shoes, and gravel might scar the polished hard floors indoors. Boots were donned to explore the garden proper. Then you could kick through a pile of rhododendron petals blown down during the morning rain, and your boots could pick up a rind of fine gravel or a dark stain of moisture from swishing along through the wet stones.

Gravel is inexpensive and easy to lay. It drains well after rain. For ease of walking, buy gravel with stones no larger than ¾ inch; smaller ones, say up to ⅜ inch, are best. A layer of landscape cloth will help prevent weeds from growing up through the path from the ground, but eventually weeds will seed into the surface; if you use the cloth, top up the gravel regularly to be sure the ugly material never shows. If you're running a gravel path up to the house, place an apron of large flagstones at the door entrance, along with a boot scraper and a stiff doormat.

People who love gravel paths are often fond of raking them, whistling the metal tines through the stones, pulling off the debris before it gets slippery and sticks to the stones, leaving crisp, clean lines and a fresh texture. Weed after a rain, when the roots come free easily.

BEDROCK SHALE AND BOULDERS

This soft gray path swings up toward the hills visible over the trees at the top end of the garden. Where the long up-slope path meets cross paths, it spreads out to the nearest boulders, and the stone slabs break the surface of the shale. It's as if the path had been cleared through a boulder-strewn hillside and the rock and grit in the bedrock had been worn down by the elements.

All the stone in this garden in fact comes from nearby quarries. Because it's local, the combination of cream boulders streaked with ochre and the flecked gray shale paths looks unquestionably natural. These are the colors in the landscape for miles around—in the church walls, the road cuts, and the bare, rocky hillsides.

HOW TO DO IT ⋞⋞⋞ This path includes a foundation of 4 inches of crushed rock—a firm base for most situations—a layer of landscape cloth (optional), and a surface of 2 inches of shale or gravel with fines. The path is edged with a metal edging strip. Use wood two-by-fours if metal edging is hard to find. In a dry climate and freely draining soil, you could lay just 2 inches of crushed rock; in poorly draining soils, lay 6 inches.

Clear any weeds, and rake the ground level. Mark out the path perimeter with the twine and stakes. Make it 4 feet wide (52 inches if you're using two-by-fours), so two people can walk along it together.

Arrange the boulders. The most natural places are on the insides or outsides of curves or at path intersections. Cluster two or three together; avoid stringing them along the path perimeter. Bury the bottom third of the boulders.

To move the large rocks into position, use a number of different tools, as necessary. You might move them on a platform (a sheet of plywood, or carpet if the rocks have moss or algae that might get scratched) sitting atop three long poles that you can then use as rollers. Use a fourth pole to lever them on and off the platform. Or secure rope or chain around the rocks, with carpet pads to help prevent scuffs, and drag them; tie a pole into the rope to turn the rocks over. Once they're in the holes, a bar is useful to turn them into exactly the right place. Never try to lift heavy rocks; instead, raise them by rolling them up a plank set on an incline. Wear strong boots and gloves, and stand clear of the rocks as you're moving them.

Dig a 6-inch trench the length and width of the path. Firm the bottom of the trench if you've disturbed the soil while digging. Place the metal edging against the sides of the trench, with its stake holes on the outside, and hammer the stakes into the ground. The edging should sit ½ inch above the surrounding soil surface. (For wooden edging, drive the stake two-by-twos into the sides of the trench, outside the twine, at intervals of 4 feet. Position the edging two-by-fours in the trench so that they protrude ½ inch above the top of the trench, and nail them to the stakes, holding or wedging the stakes firmly upright during the hammering. Saw off any protruding stakes flush with the edging.) Firm the soil against the outside of the edging.

Spread 2 inches of crushed rock into the bottom of the trench. Moisten

Moderately inexpensive
Moderately easy
Location: Sun or light shade

Tools
Rake
Measuring tape
Twine and stakes
Wheelbarrow and implements for moving
    boulders (see text)
Sturdy boots and gloves
Straight-edged spade, for digging
Metal saw for cutting metal edging or reg-
    ular saw for wooden edging
Hammer
Shovel, for spreading materials
Hose
Hand-held tamper or water-fillable roller
Measuring cup, for Stabilizer (optional)
Planting trowel

Ingredients
Boulders, local, large, 2 or 3 per 5 yards of
    path
Metal edging, with stakes, length of path
    perimeter; or redwood, heartwood
    cedar, or treated wood two-by-fours,
    plus stake two-by-twos, 12 inches
    long, 1 stake per 4 feet of perimeter,
    and nails
Crushed rock, ¾-inch, 4½ cubic feet per 1
    yard of path
Landscape cloth, 4 feet by length of path
    (optional)
Stone slabs, local, large, 3 inches thick, 1
    per 5 yards of path
Shale or gravel, ¼-inch minus with fines,
    2¼ cubic feet per 1 yard of path
Stabilizer (optional)
Snow-in-summer (Cerastium tomentosum)
    and lamb's ears (Stachys byzantina),
    16 per square yard
Pride of Madeira (Echium fastuosum), or, in
    cold climates, butterfly bush (Buddleia
    davidii), 1 per square yard

Maintenance
Water plants regularly until established;
    then less frequently
Fertilize snow-in-summer in spring
Cut or shear flowers when they fade
Rake shale regularly
Top up shale and roll every spring

this layer, and pack down the surface with the tamper or roller. Lay the next 2 inches in the same way.

Across the top of the foundation, lay a sheet of porous landscape cloth (optional), to help prevent the shale from filtering down, over time, into the foundation and weeds from growing up from the ground.

Arrange the stone slabs that will emerge through the shale. Select large, irregular, flat stones that slope gently at the sides; those, more than squares or rectangles with sawed sides, will look like they're part of the bedrock.

Spread the shale 2 inches thick. If the surface is dusty and loose, sprinkle 1 cup of Stabilizer per yard of path, and rake it in thoroughly (optional). Water the path to activate the Stabilizer. Tamp or roll the finished surface thoroughly.

Plant the snow-in-summer and lamb's ears 9 inches apart. Let them spread naturally into the path. The pride of Madeira makes a lovely contrast in height and attracts bees.

DECOMPOSED GRANITE
AND CATMINT

*Sarah Hammond, gardening teacher
and designer, passes over the brightest
gold and the blue-gray decomposed granites (d.g.) in favor of the most unobtru-
sive, ordinary kind that fades to a "nice
buff." It makes a calm, graceful, easy-
feeling space that looks warm even when
the Pacific Ocean fog slips in through the
dark cypress windbreaks.*

*A continent away, not far from the
English Channel, a friend of Sarah's,
garden writer Penelope Hobhouse, has
also planted catmint tumbling over a
d.g. path, though there they call it hog-
gin. Instead of a bench flanked with fragrant Mexican orange, the focal point is
a copper urn of ornamental grasses
placed in the center of the path on an
apron of nine bricks.*

HOW TO DO IT ⫷⫷⫷ This path includes a foundation of 4 inches of crushed rock—a firm base for most situations—a layer of landscape cloth (optional), and a surface of 2 to 3 inches of d.g. bound with Stabilizer. The path is edged with wood two-by-fours. In a dry climate and freely draining soil, you could lay just 2 inches of crushed rock; in poorly draining soils, lay 6 inches.

Clear any weeds, and rake the ground level. Mark out the path perimeter with the twine and stakes. Make it 5 feet wide, wide enough for two people to sidle along together between the flopping catmint borders.

Dig a 6-inch trench the length and width of the path. Firm the bottom of the trench if you've disturbed the soil while digging. For the neat wood edging, drive the stake two-by-twos into the sides of the trench, outside the twine, at intervals of 4 feet. Position the edging two-by-fours in the trench so that they protrude ½ inch above the top of the trench, and nail them to the stakes, holding or wedging the stakes firmly upright during the hammering. Firm the soil against the outside of the edging. Saw off any protruding stakes flush with the edging.

Spread 2 inches of crushed rock into the bottom of the trench. Moisten this layer, and pack down the surface with the tamper or roller. Lay the next 2 inches in the same way.

Across the top of the foundation, lay a sheet of porous landscape cloth (optional), to help prevent the d.g. from subsiding, over time, into the foundation and weeds from growing up from the ground.

Spread the d.g. 2 inches thick at the edges and 3 inches thick at the center, making a gentle crown. Sprinkle the d.g. with 1 cup of Stabilizer per yard of path and rake it in thoroughly. Stabilizer binds the small particles together so that the path is firmer and less muddy after rain. Water the path to activate the Stabilizer. Tamp or roll the finished surface thoroughly.

Plant the catmint 24 inches apart, 8 inches from the path edge. They'll quickly grow over the edging and bloom from mid-spring through early summer. Plant the Mexican orange (optional) 2 feet away from the ends of the bench (optional).

Inexpensive
Easy
Location: Sun or light shade

Tools
Rake
Measuring tape
Twine and stakes
Straight-edged spade, for digging
Hammer
Saw
Shovel, for spreading materials
Hose
Hand-held tamper or water-fillable roller
Measuring cup
Planting trowel

Ingredients
Redwood, heartwood cedar, or treated wood two-by-fours, for edging, length of path perimeter
Stake two-by-twos, 12 inches long, 1 stake per 4 feet of perimeter, and 3-inch nails
Crushed rock, ¾-inch, 5½ cubic feet per 1 yard of path
Landscape cloth, 5 feet by length of path (optional)
Decomposed granite (d.g.), ¼-inch minus, 3½ cubic feet per 1 yard of path
Stabilizer, small bag
Catmint (*Nepeta* 'Six Hills Giant'), 1 per 2 feet of border; or, in light shade, lady's mantle (*Alchemilla mollis*), 1 per 1½ feet
Mexican orange (*Choisya ternata*), 2 to flank bench (optional)
Bench, 4 feet long (optional)

Maintenance
Water plants regularly until established, then less frequently
Fertilize plants with slow-release fertilizer in spring
Shear dead flower spikes if unsightly; may rebloom after shearing
Cut back entire plants to 6 inches in late fall, to regrow in spring
Rake path regularly
Top up d.g. and roll every spring

HERB PARTERRE

Give a patch of herbs a wraparound gravel path, evergreen hedges, and olive trees set on the square and you've made a Mediterranean parterre. The rosemary balls at the myrtle hedge corners may grow loose and fluffy, the basil and cilantro inside the hedges will eventually turn brown and topple, and the path will keep collecting olive leaves, but still this garden will look prim. Its bones are good. The neat, formal lines follow the lines of the house and the stone terrace, against which it's been allowed to sit, unscreened.

The gravel feels deep and crunches underfoot. In the heat, fragrances rise from the myrtles and the herbs. Outside the parterre runs a thick border of English lavender, gray as the olives and the path.

HOW TO DO IT ≈≋≈ This path includes a foundation of 4 inches of crushed rock, a firm base for most situations, a layer of landscape cloth (optional), and a surface of 2 inches of gravel. The path is edged with a metal edging strip. Use wood two-by-fours if metal edging is hard to find. In a dry climate and freely draining soil, you could lay just 2 inches of crushed rock; in poorly draining soils, lay 6 inches.

Clear any weeds, and rake the ground level. Mark out the path perimeter with the twine and stakes. Make it 3 feet wide (40 inches if you're using two-by-fours). The garden consists of two herb plots separated and surrounded by the path. For a lovely flourish, scallop the two outside corners of each plot, and plant the four olives in those extra quadrants of gravel.

Dig a 6-inch trench the length and width of the path; firm the bottom of the trench if you've disturbed the soil while digging. Install the metal edging by placing it against the sides of the trench and hammering the stakes into the ground outside the trench. The edging should sit ½ inch above the surrounding soil surface. (For a wood edging, drive the stake two-by-twos into the sides of the trench, outside the twine, at intervals of 4 feet. Position the edging two-by-fours in the trench so that they protrude ½ inch above the top of the trench, and nail them to the stakes, holding or wedging the stakes firmly upright during the hammering. Saw off any protruding stakes flush with the edging.) Firm the soil against the outside of the edging.

Plant the trees (optional) to sit 2 inches higher than the finished path.

Spread 2 inches of crushed rock into the bottom of the trench. Moisten this layer, and pack down the surface with the tamper or roller. Lay the next 2 inches in the same way.

Across the top of the foundation, lay a sheet of porous landscape cloth (optional), to help prevent the gravel from filtering down, over time, into the foundation and weeds from growing up from the ground.

Spread 2 inches of gravel on the surface. Moisten this layer, and pack it down hard. Spread a thin layer of gravel over the tree rootballs, for visual continuity.

Set the rosemary plants in the corners of the herb plots, 9 inches back from the path edges. Leaving 12 inches on either side of the rosemaries, plant the myrtle hedges, spacing the plants 6 inches back from the path edge and 9 inches apart. Plant your choice of herbs in the plots. Plant the lavenders, 2 feet apart, on the outside of the parterre garden (optional).

Inexpensive
Easy
Location: Sun

Tools
Rake
Measuring tape
Twine and stakes
Straight-edged spade, for digging
Metal saw for cutting metal edging or regular saw for wooden edging
Hammer
Shovel, for spreading materials
Hose
Hand-held tamper or water-fillable roller
Planting trowel

Ingredients
Metal edging, with stakes, length of path perimeter; or redwood, heartwood cedar, or treated wood two-by-fours, plus stake two-by-twos, 12 inches long, 1 stake per 4 feet of perimeter, and nails
Olives (Olea europaea), nonfruiting, multi-stemmed, or, in cold climates, apple trees, 1 per corner (optional)
Crushed rock, ¾-inch, 3¼ cubic feet per 1 yard of path
Landscape cloth, 3 feet by length of path (optional)
Gravel, gray, crushed not round, ¼- to ⅜-inch, 1¾ cubic feet per 1 yard of path; in cold climates, consider a warm-colored gravel
Rosemaries (Rosmarinus officinalis), 1 per corner
Dwarf myrtles (Myrtus communis 'Compacta'), 4 per 1 yard of hedge
Herbs, a mixture with contrasting foliages
Lavenders (Lavendula angustifolia) (optional)

Maintenance
Water olives and hedges regularly until established, then only during dry season
Water herbs according to plant labels
Trim hedges and rosemaries twice a year
Prune olives every two years, until mature
Rake gravel regularly
Top up gravel as necessary

BASALT AND LIME-GOLD SLOPE

This path zigzags across a hillside on the edge of Lake Washington. From a bluestone terrace with views over old conifers to the water, it cuts down away from the drama into the peace of a densely planted garden. The gravel is a uniform, dark, northwest mountain basalt gray, the plantings airy and golden. On a thundery afternoon, a tiny breeze that causes no stirrings in the firs sets the thin leaves of the golden robinia trees at the top of the path trembling and swaying in huge, bright drifts of lime green and gold. The same airy movement and lightness ripple down the path—in the long, bouncing stems of delicate white gaura flowers and chartreuse nicotiana, the white and pale lemon cinquefoil on the banks, and the green-gold marjoram and felty, thick, gray lamb's ears seeding across the gravel, connecting the bank and the downslope.

HOW TO DO IT ≈≈≈ This path includes a foundation of 4 inches

of crushed rock—a firm base for most situations—and a surface of 2 inches of crushed basalt. A stone step is set into the path to ease the gradient. In a dry climate and freely draining soil, you could lay just 2 inches of crushed rock. In poorly draining soils, lay 6 inches of crushed rock, but consult a landscape architect about drainage and erosion if the slope is steep.

Cut out of the hillside a 5-foot-wide swath for the path, carefully removing any topsoil and storing it off to one side. Slope the path gently across its width; make it 1 inch lower on the downhill side. Through the length of the path, the drop should be no greater than 1 foot over 8 feet. To avoid a steeper gradient, cut out a 6-inch-deep step, and continue to grade below it. To check the gradient, place one end of the long board at the top of the slope, walk down the slope with the other end of it, and rest it on top of the 1-foot pole. Place the level on the long board and move the pole up or down the path until the board is level. Measure the distance from the top of the path to the pole to see how many feet of path it took for the gradient to fall 1 foot. Continue measuring to the bottom of the path.

Cut the whole path out of the hillside; don't build the path on fill, because it won't hold. On a steep hillside, grade beyond the path edges to ensure that the uphill bank doesn't slide onto the path or the downhill edge slide down the slope. As a rule of thumb, the banks will hold if they slope no more than 1 foot over 3 feet, though the angle of repose for your slope depends on soil type and how much water is running off it. Retain the edges with sturdy timber boards and deep stakes if necessary. Plant the newly graded banks as soon as possible, to help prevent erosion. Consult a landscape architect if your slope is steep or unstable or if rainwater courses down it in channels. Keep the grade unchanged around trees; they'll die, slowly over many years, if their roots are exposed or more deeply buried.

Mark out the path perimeter with the twine and stakes. Make it 4 feet wide, 6 inches in from the bank and 6 inches back from the downslope. Dig a 6-inch trench the length and width of the path; firm the bottom of the trench if you've disturbed the soil while digging.

Lay the foundation first in the lowest stretch of path, going as far as the step. As you spread and tamp the materials, work from the bottom of the slope up, so the materials lock against each other. Spread 2 inches of crushed

Inexpensive
Moderately easy
Location: Sun

Tools
Straight-edged spade, for digging
Measuring tape
Straight piece of board, 8 feet long, for measuring gradient
Pole, or piece of two-by-four, 1 foot long, for measuring gradient
Level
Twine and stakes
Shovel, for spreading materials
Hose
Hand-held tamper or water-fillable roller
Planting trowel

Ingredients
Crushed rock, ¾-inch, 4½ cubic feet per 1 yard of path
Stone slab for step, approx. 12 inches wide, 4 feet long, 7 inches deep, split into two for easier handling
Crushed basalt or other gray gravel, ⅝-inch minus, 2¼ cubic feet per 1 yard of path
A mix of airy perennials, shrubs, and ground covers, such as pale yellow cinquefoil (*Potentilla fruticosa* 'Primrose Beauty'); blue lily-of-the-Nile (*Agapanthus* Headbourne hybrids) or, in cold climates, forget-me-nots (*Myosotis sylvatica*); gaura (*Gaura lindheimeri*); nicotiana (*Nicotiana langsdorfii*); lamb's ears (*Stachys byzantina*); golden marjoram (*Origanum vulgare* 'Aureum')
Gold-foliaged tree, such as *Robinia pseudoacacia* 'Frisia'
Large shrubs and small trees, such as narrow conifers, viburnums, mountain ash (*Sorbus* spp.) (optional)

Maintenance
Water plants regularly until established, then less frequently
Fertilize plants in spring
Stake gaura if it becomes unwieldy
Rake gravel regularly
Top up gravel as necessary

rock into the bottom of the trench. Moisten this layer, and pack down the surface with the tamper or roller. Lay the next 2 inches in the same way.

Place the pieces of stone slab on the top of the step, tilting them gently downslope, so puddles don't collect on the step. Lay the crushed rock in the next stretch of path, 2 inches at a time, as before.

On top of the rock, spread the crushed basalt 2 inches deep, working from the bottom of the path. Again, moisten this layer, and pack it down hard.

Plant the banks and the path edges. Place the cinquefoil, lily-of-the-Nile, gaura, and nicotiana about 2 feet back from the path edge, and the lamb's ears and golden marjoram at the path edge. Plant the golden robinia tree or a smaller gold-foliaged tree, shrub, or vine as a focal point. Disguise the downslope beyond these with plantings of large shrubs and small trees (optional). The path feels more secluded and the drop less intimidating if you can't see the next stretch zigzagging below.

WHITE AND GRAY CHIPS, SEEDS, AND GRASSES

Gold rudbeckias and blue asters are bursting open in spray after spray of flamboyant late-August color, but the garden is changing already from flower to seed. Buff and raspberry-red seeded drumsticks have started to topple onto the path, and the fluffy seed plumes of the grasses are turning from purple to beige. Once a severe frost knocks out the last of the asters, the garden will become a study in soft winter elegance: a clicking, sharp, white-and-steel-gray crushed granite path, billowy dun yellow grasses with tall, buff seed wands, black rudbeckia cones on bristly chocolate brown stalks, occasional winter sunbeams sparkling on the white chips in the gravel, the seeds all now dropped into the earth, and the hollow stalks and grasses rattling and whispering in the wind.

HOW TO DO IT ❧❧❧ This path includes a foundation of 4 inches of crushed rock—a firm base for most situations—a layer of landscape cloth (optional), and a surface of 2 inches of gravel. The path is edged with a metal edging strip. Use wood two-by-fours if metal edging is hard to find. In a dry climate and freely draining soil, you could lay just 2 inches of crushed rock; in poorly draining soils, lay 6 inches.

Clear any weeds, and rake the ground level. Mark out the path perimeter with the twine and stakes. Make it a broad, elegant 6 feet wide (76 inches if you're using two-by-fours) to allow for the arching grasses.

Dig a 6-inch trench the length and width of the path; firm the bottom of the trench if you've disturbed the soil while digging. Install the metal edging by placing it against the sides of the trench and hammering the stakes into the ground outside the trench. The edging should sit ½ inch above the surrounding soil surface. (For a wood edging, drive the stake two-by-twos into the sides of the trench, outside the twine, at intervals of 4 feet. Position the edging two-by-fours in the trench so that they protrude ½ inch above the top of the trench, and nail them to the stakes, holding or wedging the stakes firmly upright during the hammering. Saw off any protruding stakes flush with the edging. Use several layers of benderboard for curves; nail the layers together, staggering the joints, and nail the set to the stakes in the ground.) Firm the soil against the outside of the edging.

Spread 2 inches of crushed rock into the bottom of the trench. Moisten this layer, and pack down the surface with the tamper or roller. Lay the next 2 inches in the same way.

Across the top of the rock, lay a sheet of porous landscape cloth (optional), to help prevent the gravel from filtering down, over time, into the foundation and weeds from growing up from the ground.

Spread 2 inches of gravel on the surface. Moisten this layer, and pack it down hard.

Inexpensive
Easy
Location: Sun

Tools
Rake
Measuring tape
Twine and stakes
Straight-edged spade, for digging
Metal saw for cutting metal edging or
    regular saw for wooden edging
Hammer
Shovel, for spreading materials
Hose
Hand-held tamper or water-fillable roller
Planting trowel

Ingredients
Metal edging, with stakes, length of path
    perimeter; or redwood, heartwood
    cedar, or treated wood two-by-fours
    plus stake two-by-twos, 12 inches
    long, 1 stake per 4 feet of perimeter;
    benderboard for curves
Crushed rock, ¾-inch, 6½ cubic feet per
    1 yard of path
Landscape cloth, 6 feet by length of path
    (optional)
Gravel, crushed granite, ⅜-inch, no fines,
    3¼ cubic feet per 1 yard of path
Fountain grasses (*Pennisetum
    alopecuroides*), 1 per 4 feet of path
    perimeter
Rudbeckias (*Rudbeckia fulgida*
    'Goldsturm'), 5 or 7 per 5 yards of
    path
Asters (*Aster frikartii*), 5 or 7 per 5 yards
    of path
Drumsticks (*Allium sphaerocephalum*), 5
    per 1 yard of path
Coral bells (*Heuchera micrantha* 'Ruby
    Veil'), 2 per 1 yard of path
Creeping thyme (*Thymus praecox arcticus*),
    2 per 1 yard of path

Maintenance
Water grasses and thyme regularly until
    established, then only in dry season
Water other plants regularly
Fertilize flower plants in spring
Remove spent aster flowers, to keep
    plants flowering
Divide asters in late fall; replant pieces
    from outside of plant
Divide rudbeckias and coral bells every
    three years
Rake gravel regularly
Top up gravel as necessary

Set the fountain grasses 4 feet apart along the path, 2 feet back from the edge. Plant the rudbeckias and asters behind the grasses in sweeps of five or seven, 18 inches between plants. Plant the drumstick bulbs in fall between the grasses in groups of five, 9 inches apart. Plant the coral bells in front of the grasses, at the path edge; alternate them with the creeping thyme.

STONE

Stones taken straight out of a hillside or riverbed are a paradise of natural irregularity: rippled, veined, stippled, dimpled, jagged, domed, dotted with mosses and lichens, duff brown or slate gray or blond with iron streaks. Placed back into the local landscape — as bumpy fieldstone paths following the contours of a hillside garden or as stepping-stones bridging wet grass — they blend with the bedrock, and the paths are guaranteed to look timeless and simple.

Japanese gardeners four hundred years ago chose irregular stones for the stepping-stone walk to the tea hut. They sought out stones whose imperfect shapes spoke to one another, a curve on one stone flowing into a hollow on its neighbor. The sizes of the stones were purposefully varied, and the asymmetric pattern of the path on the ground was carefully designed so that the rhythm of the steps would lead the mind to pause.

Once stone is split or sawed into straight shapes, it loses its rusticity. Flagstone in large, uniform rectangles laid end to end is unreservedly formal and grand. The hard edges and subtle variations in color and texture luxuriously complement soft foliage, sun-bleached wooden benches, or stone water troughs stained with algae. Being so elegant and yet natural, cut stone makes an appropriate bridge between a large, formal house and the landscape: the polished floors indoors continue over the threshold onto a smooth stone that weathers gently to the colors in the hillsides.

Exotic stone, brought in from a different landscape, makes a bold path. The less it looks like local stone, the more ostentatious it will be. Check the color of the stone when it's wet and when it's dry. Since it won't blend into the natural landscape, make sure it works with the colors of your house and the plants in your garden.

Stone is expensive, perhaps prohibitively so if it needs to come far. See what's available from local quarries, how it's cut, whether it crumbles or cracks as it weathers, whether it stains easily. Look for some roughness even in formal flagstone slabs, so that they're not slippery in rain. Spread sand over stone paths in winter to improve traction. Build a wide path if you can, to leave room at the edges for slippery hummocks of spongy moss or blisters of orange lichen to grow over the stone.

BEACH TRAIL WITH POPPIES OF RHODES

Poppies of Rhodes grow close in a low thicket huddled away from the salt wind. The yellow petals beat all day against the sand and driftwood and water-washed stones, but then in the lull at sunset suddenly fall still, varnished gold in front of the silver sea. Mornings, there's a chill on the stones; whirls of old poppy petals have blown in the night under the driftwood, and skinny seed pods, long as horns, are where the petals once were.

The sea lavender spikes rise from rings of leathery leaves in spring and last all through summer, upright and stiff in the breeze. Sunroses sprawl along the warm sand, on the leeward side of other plants or driftwood, blooming and reblooming like the poppies, tickling the edges of the stones.

HOW TO DO IT ≋≋≋

This path has no foundation. The heavy stones are settled directly on top of the soil, their surfaces 2 inches above grade. They may shift a little over time but are easily resettled. If your soil freezes hard or drains poorly, lay 4 inches of crushed rock, 2 inches of gravel, and 2 inches of sand below each stone.

Choose the stones carefully. Those with lovely, rounded outlines may not have the flattest surfaces, but that's all right, especially if it's a short path; people will pick up on the unevenness quickly and slow down. In rainy or icy climates, reject stones with concavities in the center, where the tread will be. They might fill with water and prove treacherous.

Clear any weeds, and rake the ground level. Lay out the stones, with roughly 4-inch gaps between them. Place the threshold stone as a landing at

the start of the path and plan to put the other stones in a pattern that's pleasing to you. Snake the path gently, aiming it at a position one yard to the right of the destination and then jagging it over quickly with the last few stones. Once you have a path line that flows a little, imagine a piece of string down the center of it; lay the stones so they zigzag off this line. Stones laid one behind the other, centers aligned, look military. Orient each stone so that its longest side lies across the path, the steps more broad than deep, like a stairway. Study the outline of each stone. Designers, and trained Japanese gardeners, will lay a stone with a bulging side alongside a stone with an indented side. The path flows beautifully then.

Once the stones are in place, settle them into the ground one at a time. If the soil is soft and sandy, you may be able to wedge and screw the stones into their settled positions. In heavier soils, roll the stone aside and dig out a trench with the trowel. Make sure all the stones are firm underfoot before planting the flowers.

Plant the poppies on either side of the path, 18 inches apart, 18 inches back

Moderately inexpensive
Easy
Location: Sun

Tools
Rake
Planting trowel
Hose or watering can

Ingredients
Stepping-stones with round edges, 3 or 4
    inches thick, at least 18 inches across,
    approx. 2 per 1 yard of path
Threshold stone, approx. 2 by 3 feet
Poppies of Rhodes (*Glaucium flavum*), 4
    per 1 yard of path
Sea lavenders (*Limonium perezii* or, in
    harsh-winter climates, hardier species),
    1 per 1 yard of path
Sunroses (*Helianthemum nummularium*),
    yellow variety, 1 per 1 yard of path, or
    in harsh-winter climates, evening prim-
    rose (*Oenothera* spp.)
Beach sand, approx. ½ cubic foot per
    1 yard of path
Large pebbles, driftwood

Maintenance
Water plants regularly until they are
    established, then only lightly
Shear sunroses after flowering, so they
    rebloom
Cut poppies back to basal leaves in late
    fall, when seeds have dropped
Rake and top up sand occasionally
In harsh winters, protect sunroses with
    evergreen boughs, and, if poppies die,
    wait for new plants to grow from their
    seeds

from the stones. Plant the sea lavenders and sunroses in just a few gaps, leaving most of the gaps unplanted, to show off the sand and the stones.

Scatter a ½-inch layer of fine beach sand between the stones and into the plantings on either side. For ornaments along the path edges, collect large, egg-shaped pebbles and bone-smooth or gnarled or fire-blackened driftwood. Be aware that it is illegal to remove these objects, and sand, from some public beaches. Check with authorities first.

STEPPING-STONE BRIDGE ACROSS MEADOW

The countryside has been allowed to creep in all the way to the front door. In the entrance court, between stepping-stones, daisies and cranesbills and violets have sprung up thickly, delicate as hedgerow flowers. On the slope alongside the house, common yarrow grows thick as a lawn. The stepping-stone path is the only way across it when it's left unmowed in spring and summer and grows into a meadow of tall, soft, ferny wildflowers, pink, white, and cream.

HOW TO DO IT ⋙ The stepping-stones are laid on 2-inch pads of concrete, to hold them firmly on the slope. If your soil freezes hard or drains poorly, lay 4 inches of crushed rock or gravel below the concrete. If your path is not on a slope, lay a base of 2 inches of sand, instead of concrete. The stones are laid flush with the lawn, so that a mower will pass over them without catching. (In some areas yarrow can become invasive; contain it with a strong edging if necessary.)

Clear any weeds, and rake the ground level. Lay out the stones at a comfortable distance from one another (maybe 6 to 9 inches) in an elongated S: start the swing at the beginning of the path, leading it away from the adjoining area at a gentle angle. Continue the swing out toward a point where the eye might rest—in this garden it's a white calla and later a white rose, Iceberg, that's repeated along the other paths in the garden—then gently curve the path back toward another focal point—here it's an oak with boulders to sit on in the shade. Adjust the stones until the path seems to flow naturally.

Position the threshold stone at the start of the path. Orient each stone so that its longest side lies across the path, the steps more broad than deep, like a stairway. If a stone breaks, lay the two pieces alongside each other with a 2-inch gap between, so that it looks intentional.

Start at the downhill end of the path if it slopes, and work uphill. Mark around the edges of the stones with the knife and move the stones off to the side. Excavate to the depth of the stone plus 2 inches. With the back of the spade or the tamper, firm and level the bottom of the hole.

Put on the rubber gloves to keep the cement off your skin. In the bucket or wheelbarrow, prepare a batch of concrete according to the directions on the bag. Add the water slowly, and turn the mix thoroughly with a hoe.

Shovel a 2-inch layer of concrete into the first hole. Wet the sponge in the bucket of water, and wipe the base of the first stone clean. With the trowel, spread concrete onto the wet underside of the stone, then scrape it off, back into the mixing bucket, stir the mix around, and spread another scoop across the base of the stone. Settle the stone into the wet concrete pad, flush with the soil level. Immediately wash off any smears of concrete on the surface of the stone. Make the concrete pad for the next stone, and so on, until you've completed the path. Let the concrete set for at least a few hours before preparing the soil for the plants.

Inexpensive
Moderately easy
Location: Sun

Tools
Rake
Knife, for marking stone shapes
Straight-edged spade, for digging
Measuring tape
Hand-held tamper (optional)
Rubber gloves
Concrete-mixing bucket or wheelbarrow
Hose or watering can
Hoe, for mixing concrete
Household sponge
Bucket of water
Planting trowel, for yarrow six-packs and
    (optional) flower plants
Rotary cultivator, for yarrow (optional)
Roller, for yarrow seed
Seed spreader, for yarrow seed (optional)

Ingredients
Threshold stone, approx. 3 by 2 feet
Stepping-stones, approx. 18 by 24 inches,
    4 per 3 yards of path
Ready-mix concrete, approx. ½ cubic foot
    per stone
Daisies (*Erigeron karvinskianus* or *Bellis
    perennis*), cranesbills (*Geranium* spp.),
    violets (*Viola* spp.) (optional)
Builder's sand, for sowing yarrow seed,
    small bag
Common yarrow (*Achillea millefolium*),
    16 plants per square yard of planting
    area, or 3 ounces of seed per 500
    square feet

Maintenance
Water yarrow regularly until it is established, then only in dry season
Fertilize yarrow twice during growing
    season (optional)
Mow yarrow every 6 weeks to 6 months
    with rotary mower

Plant daisies, cranesbills, and violets around the first few stepping-stones (optional).

Make the yarrow lawn in one of two ways. The more expensive way is to buy six-packs or flats and plant the young plants 9 inches apart. The economical, and less time-consuming, way is to sow seed in fall or spring. For either method, dig or rototill the ground to a depth of 4 inches, and rake it level. If the soil is loose and fluffy, tamp it or roll it.

Either plant the young plants, or mix the seed with an equal amount of sand and sow the mix over the soil surface. To sow the seed evenly by hand, do a dummy run with only sand, until you develop a swinging motion and pace that produce an even cover. Alternatively, rent a seed spreader. Make one pass over the seeded area with a roller; to germinate well, the seeds need to be in good contact with the soil and also exposed to light, so don't bury them. Water the area gently.

Mow in early spring and after flowering, or as often as every six weeks. Set the mower blades at 4 inches. A tighter cut and infrequent mowing leave the yarrow looking brown for a week.

CUT STONE AND MYRTLE SPHERES

One long, grand view runs all the way from the front door, through several large rooms and a central courtyard in the house, out the French doors, into the garden. Compared with the house, the garden is small. The path, and the garden, ends a couple of feet from here, in a border of lavender, at the pool. But the scale is oversize, and the decoration supersimple, so the space registers as absolutely gracious and generous. The path is almost as wide as a terrace, so there's space to spare for aromatic myrtle topiary spheres in large pots, lined up in rows to stretch out the sight line.

HOW TO DO IT ⁂ This path is laid on a foundation of 4 inches of gravel and 2 inches of sand, a firm, long-lasting base suitable for most situations. If your soil freezes hard or drains poorly, lay 4 inches of crushed rock (1½-inch), a layer of landscape cloth, 2 inches of gravel, and 2 inches of sand. The slabs are laid tight, without gaps. Those on the path edge are spot-mortared for stability. The path base is contained by an edging of two-by-fours, sunk just below the path surface. In cold-winter climates, lay the slabs with ¼-inch gaps, so the stone can expand and contract without cracking. In rainy climates, build up the center of the path just a little, so rain will drain off to both sides. Be aware that some kinds of stone stain easily; don't use these near trees or shrubs with messy fruits.

Draw out the configuration of the slabs on graph paper. The 18-by-36 slabs run lengthwise along the sides of the path. Mark in the 36-by-24 slabs next; zigzag them up the central panel. Then fill in the gaps with the smaller slabs. Rearrange as necessary to avoid a cluster of small slabs. Check how much variation there is in the cutting of the stones; if they're cut a bit larger than specified, you may need to have one or two re-sawed to make them fit. Identify any oversize stones, and plan to lay those at the first opportunity.

Clear any weeds, and rake the ground level. Mark out the path perimeter with the twine and stakes; make it 8½ feet wide. Dig a 9-inch trench the length and width of the path. Firm the bottom of the trench if you've disturbed the soil while digging.

Spread 2 inches of gravel into the bottom of the trench. Moisten this layer, and pack down the surface with the tamper or roller. Lay the next 2 inches in the same way.

For the wood edging, drive the stake one-by-twos into the sides of the trench, inside the twine, at intervals of 4 feet, the 2-inch side flush with the trench sides. Rest the edging two-by-fours in the trench, on the gravel, and check that the path width between the wood edgings is exactly 8 feet. Nail the two-by-fours to the stakes, holding or wedging the stakes firmly upright during the hammering. Firm the soil against the outside of the edging. Saw off any protruding stakes flush with the edging.

On top of the gravel, spread 2 inches of sand. Dampen the sand, tamp it, level it, and tamp again. Check with the level that the sand bed is even.

Moderately expensive
Moderately difficult
Location: Sun or light shade

Tools
Graph paper and pencil
Rake
Measuring tape
Twine and stakes
Straight-edged spade, for digging
Shovel, for spreading materials
Hose
Hand-held tamper or water-fillable roller
Hammer
Saw
Level
Rubber gloves
Bucket or wheelbarrow, for mixing mortar
Builder's trowel, triangular
Rubber mallet
Straight two-by-four, 6 feet long
Paintbrush, to apply sealant (optional)
Broom
Planting trowel

Ingredients
Gravel, sharp-edged, ⅝- or ¾-inch, 2 cubic
    yards per 6 yards of path
Two-by-fours, for edging, length of path
    perimeter
Stake one-by-twos, 12 inches long, 1 stake
    per 4 feet of perimeter, and 3-inch
    nails
Builder's sand, 1¼ cubic yards per 6 yards
    of path
Ready-mix mortar, small bag
Cut stone, 2 inches thick, rough textured
    for safety, 144 square feet per 6 yards
    of path, composed of
        12 slabs, 18 by 36 inches, for edges
        5 slabs, 24 by 36 inches
        7 slabs, 24 by 24 inches
        7 slabs, 12 by 24 inches
        18 slabs, 12 by 12 inches
Stone sealant, porous, natural finish, not
    shiny (optional)
8 terra-cotta pots, 18-inch or larger
Potting soil, approx. 3 bags
Myrtles (Myrtus communis), 1 per pot

Maintenance
Water pots regularly
Clip myrtles into balls, early spring and fall
Check annually for heaving of slabs, and
    reset if necessary
Clean light-colored stone, as necessary

Put on rubber gloves to keep the cement off your skin, and mix the wet mortar in the bucket or wheelbarrow. Add water according to the instructions on the bag. Line up the large 18-by-36 slabs along the sides of the path.

Starting at one corner of the path, scoop up six fist-sized dollops of mortar with the trowel, and deposit them on the sand where the first large edging slab will lie. Spread and furrow the mortar spots until they're about 1 inch thick. Place the slab on top of the mortar, outside edges absolutely straight against the edging. Tap the slab with the mallet. Use the level to make sure it's even. Lay all the slabs down one side of the path in the same way, without gaps between them, stones protruding above the wood edging. Lay the second side, using the level across the 6-foot two-by-four to be sure the stones are flush with the first side. Clean the mortar off the tools before it hardens.

Lay the center of the path without mortar. Spread about 1 inch more sand over the original sand bed so that the slabs will sit flush with those mortared along the path edge. Moisten the sand, tamp it, and check that the sand bed is level. Settle each slab as you lay it by tapping it with the mallet. Using the level, check that it's flush with the slabs on the path sides; if necessary, lift the slab and spread more sand underneath it.

When the path is laid, paint a stone sealant onto the stones (optional) if they are light colored and likely to stain easily. Choose a porous product that will not leave a shine or discolor the stone.

Sweep dry sand over the stones and into the cracks, to within ¼ inch of the path surface. Stand on the central panel, not the mortared edges, which need a week to set firm. Sprinkle the path with a hose to settle the sand, then top up the cracks with a second sweep of sand, and sprinkle again.

When the path edges are firm, cover the wood edging with soil or whatever surface borders the path, and plant the myrtle bushes in the pots.

FIELDSTONES AND IRISES

Harmony is found mainly in old gardens, a result of old-fashioned making do. One variety of iris to flower in spring, then one variety of daisy or gray lamb's ears for the summer; the plants are set out alternately along the path, making a plain, restful rhythm. And for the path surface, nothing exotic or imported, just the small, round stones dug and tumbled and raked out of the hillside.

The materials are simple, but there's art in the details. The path flows like water under the trees, now wide and pooling in a low stretch, now narrow and twisting, roiling up over a hump, and round again to another pool. The decoration consists of a domed stone here and there on the bends. A flat, oblong landing and an obelisk mark the path entrance. The litter between the hard, uneven stones has simple country texture: brittle leaves, white as ash, dark berries from the trees, daisy seedlings.

HOW TO DO IT ≋≋≋

This path has no foundation and no edging. The stones are packed tightly together in a trench, on top of soil. The path will shift and heave naturally. If your soil freezes hard or drains poorly, make a firm foundation: excavate to 12 inches and lay 4 inches of crushed rock (1½-inch), a layer of landscape cloth, 2 inches of gravel, and 2 inches of sand.

Clear any weeds, and rake the ground level. Mark out the path perimeter with the twine and stakes; make it approximately 3 feet wide, wider at the entrance and the destination and where it swings around a gentle bend, narrower in one or two spots, to create interest. Snake the path, aiming it first at a position 2 yards to the left of the destination, then 1 yard to the right of the destination, and jagging it over in the last couple of yards.

Dig a 4-inch trench the length and width of the path. Leave some of the soil alongside the path edges, to pack around the stones. If there's any slope on the path, start work at the base of the slope and work uphill.

Place the large threshold stone as a landing at the start of the path. Pack the other stones around it, as close as you can wedge them, flattest sides up. Wedge the thicker stones down into the soil, excavating the trench a little deeper if necessary. Pack extra soil underneath the shallower stones to support them. Lay the flattest stones in the path center.

After laying a 2-foot stretch of path, fill the gaps between the stones with soil, packing it down hard with the trowel to lock the stones together. Spread a ½-inch layer of gravel over the soil (optional).

Place the boulders in the flower beds. Bury the bottom third of the boulders. Position the obelisk stone to one side of the path entrance. Dig a hole to bury at least one-third of it, to ensure that it's stable.

Plant the irises 1 foot apart in clumps of five along the path edges. Repeat the clumps, irregularly, down the path. Stagger the other plants in the same way.

Moderately inexpensive
Easy
Location: Sun or light shade

Tools
Rake
Twine and stakes
Straight-edged spade, for digging
Planting trowel
Shovel, for spreading gravel (optional)
Hose or watering can

Ingredients
Threshold stone, approximately 1 by 2 feet
Fieldstones with worn round edges, 6 to 9 inches across, approx. 25 per 1 yard of path
Gravel, ⅜-inch minus, approx. ¼ cubic foot per 1 yard of path (optional)
Boulders, 2 or 3, for flower beds
Obelisk stone, for entrance
Bearded irises, blue, 5 per clump
Lamb's ears (Stachys byzantina), blue marguerites (Felicia amelloides), blue fescues (Festuca ovina 'Glauca'), euphorbias, pink oxalis, and Mexican daisies (Erigeron karvinskianus) to fill beds

Maintenance
Water plants regularly until established, then less frequently
Remove old leaves from irises in fall
Divide irises every 3 or 4 years

MEDITERRANEAN CRAZY PAVING

The stone path pauses in a circle with curving stone-topped benches and a bank of Iceberg roses and English lavenders. The air is still and warm in the shelter of the bank, so the oils from the flower petals and the thyme foliage on the floor evaporate into heavy fragrances that hang close. This is crazy paving done the original Roman way: rich decoration, stone architecture, stone floor.

Crazy paving can be fussy. The late British garden designer Russell Page couldn't comprehend what drove "even quite sophisticated amateurs to smash good paving slabs into fragments and, like Hansel and Gretel in the fairy-tale, scatter trails of them across the garden." But, if you cover every sharp edge of each stone with the thyme and keep the scale grand, instead of a trail of small bits your path will read as an expensive hard stone floor with a fragrant, soft carpet.

HOW TO DO IT ❧❧❧

This path is laid on a foundation of 3 inches of gravel and 3 inches of sand, a firm, long-lasting base suitable for most situations. If your soil freezes hard or drains poorly, lay 4 inches of crushed rock (1½-inch), a layer of landscape cloth, 2 inches of gravel, and 3 inches of sand. The path has no edging; if your path is on unstable soil or slopes, install a metal or benderboard edging (see page 59) to contain the path base.

Clear any weeds, and rake the ground level. Mark out the path perimeter with the twine and stakes; make it 5 feet wide. (If you're making a circle, make it 17 feet across, to allow for a 7-foot center bed of lavenders or roses or daylilies or a stone water feature.)

Dig a 7-inch trench the length and width of the path. Firm the bottom of the trench if you've disturbed the soil while digging. Spread 3 inches of gravel into the trench, and compact it with the tamper or roller. On top of the gravel, lay 3 inches of sand. Dampen the sand, tamp it, level it, and tamp again. Check with the level that the sand bed is even.

Arrange the stones in the sand bed. For a pleasing pattern, distribute the sizes fairly evenly, in particular avoiding a cluster of small stones. Leave 3-inch gaps between the stones for the thyme. Bed each stone firmly into the sand, tapping it in several places with the mallet. Using the level, check that it's flush with the rest of the path; if necessary, lift the stone and spread more sand underneath it.

When the stones are laid, sweep a 50:50 mix of dry sand and potting soil into the gaps, filling them to within 1 inch of the path surface. Water the path to settle the soil.

Plant the thyme in the gaps and at the path edges. Space the plants 6 inches apart. Keep the soil lower than the path surface so that it doesn't wash over the stones. Plant the lavenders and roses 3 feet apart in staggered rows.

Moderately expensive
Moderately easy
Location: Sun or shade

Tools
Rake
Measuring tape
Twine and stakes
Straight-edged spade, for digging
Shovel, for spreading materials
Hand-held tamper or water-fillable roller
Hose
Level
Rubber mallet
Broom
Planting trowel

Ingredients
Gravel, sharp-edged, ⅜-inch, 4 cubic feet per 1 yard of path
Builder's sand, 4¼ cubic feet per 1 yard of path
Flagstones, irregular shapes, at least 15 inches across, minimum 1½ inches thick, 12 square feet per 1 yard of path
Potting soil, approx. 1 bag per 5 yards of path
Woolly thyme (*Thymus pseudolanuginosus*), or, in deep shade, baby's tears (*Soleirolia soleirolii*), small plants in flats, approx. 25 per 1 yard of path
English lavenders (*Lavandula angustifolia*)
Iceberg roses

Maintenance
Water thyme frequently until established and full, then less frequently
Clip growing tips of thyme to restrain from covering entire stones

GRASS AND WOOD

A grass path in the morning holds cold, fresh dew that evaporates with a scent of damp earth. Later, if the day turns warm, the path will smell of summer, clover, hayseed. When every other path in the garden is as hot as a tin roof, grass is cool enough to walk on barefoot. It's tickly when it's mowed back tight to stubble, and soft when it grows out emerald green and full of shadow.

A rich, deep-green grass path suggests a natural garden with an abundance of sunlight and moisture. Running between the herb garden and the flower beds and lawn areas, it turns the garden into one seamless spread of verdant growth. Grass paths that have been cut through meadows, or through unmowed lawns away from the house, merge the garden with the countryside, drawing in the views and opening up places for planting ornamental grasses and wildflowers.

Paths of sawdust and bark look and smell best in shade, where moisture drips off a bank or from overhanging foliage and keeps the path a dark duff-brown, scented with the smells of sap and woodland rot. Like grass paths, wood paths blend into the garden, creating a natural, easy-feeling space. They turn the color of rich garden soil, tree stumps, split-rail fences, and shingles. Bark and sawdust paths wear and sag in the middle like true woodland trails; they crumble eventually into dust or wash into the flower beds, mulching the flowers generously as the wood rots away. In contrast, railroad ties make a solid, plain, outdoor floor that will last. Lay them in a chunky pattern of thick, broad stripes with thin stripes of wood-land flowers between.

Grass and wood paths are the least expensive to build. They work well on slopes, and their shapes may be changed easily. Keep grass paths open and passable in wet winters with a string of raised stepping-stones. In arid climates, a gravel path will blend better with the landscape than a grass path and be easier to maintain. In partial shade, creeping red fescue grows better than other grasses. The shaggy cowlicks of the fescue path in the photograph on page 82 have never been cut.

TALL LAWN WITH NARCISSUS, MOWED CIRCLE

Between the tall wild lawn and the stone entrance, a circle of clean, green mowing stripes spins out under an old walnut tree. It's tempting to delay arriving and follow the mowing lines into the swaying shadow of the tree canopy and the flickering light that pierces its huge round head. A few twigs have tumbled down into the circle since the last mowing. A breeze riffles in across the farm pasture, catches at the ornamental grasses patched into the stone entrance, and whistles across the troughs and glistening crests of the unmowed lawn dotted with narcissus in spring.

HOW TO DO IT 〰〰〰 This grass path is mowed through an exist-ing lawn planted with narcissus. To start a lawn from seed, follow the instruc-tions at the end of this recipe.

Mark out with the twine and stakes the perimeter of the swath to be mowed. On flat ground, choose a shape that mimics a major element in the garden, such as a tree canopy, roof line, or fence line; or make an abstract shape. On undulating ground, mark out a swath that follows the lay of the land, emphasizing its slopes and folds; it will look particularly natural if you think of it as water and let it flow just where water would, over the lowest dip in the hill line, at the foot of slopes, around outcrops and banks.

Mow the area you've marked out. Set the blades low (check the recom-mended mowing height for your grass), and mow in opposite directions to create a ribbed pattern. Remove the clippings for a neat, clean shape next to an entrance. Mow the swath often, to keep it green and healthy.

Allow the rest of the lawn to grow tall. The unmowed grasses in the pho-tograph are 1 foot tall. Mow this area as seldom as once or twice a year or every six weeks, as you prefer. Always set the blades on the highest setting. If you mow it just once a year, the grass will be yellow as a straw field for a week or two after the mowing.

Close to the house, plant the large, graceful ornamental grasses such as maiden grass or fountain grass (optional). Space them 4 feet apart in grand arcs, and in fall plant the narcissus bulbs 6 inches deep, 3 per square foot, in similar sweeps in the unmowed lawn grass (don't mow the long grass until the narcissus leaves die back after flowering). Lift a few stones from the entrance, and plant small, delicate grasses in the pockets (optional).

To start a successful lawn from seed: First choose the seed mix that best suits your climate and the amount of shade on the site. The grass needs to be a durable kind. You might choose a native grass mix for the unmowed lawn and a finer mix for the mowed path. Check the recommended time to start the seedbed; some grasses do better if started in late summer, some if started in spring. Prepare the ground carefully. Clear the area of weeds, water it, wait for any weed seeds to germinate or roots to resprout, remove them, and repeat this process until the area is clean. Spread 2 inches of weed-free com-post or manure over the area and a high-phosphate lawn-starter fertilizer. If you have any reason to think your soil is unusually acid or alkaline, have the

Inexpensive
Easy
Location: Sun or light shade

Tools
Twine and stakes
Lawn mower
Planting trowel
Hose or watering can

For a lawn from seed
Hose
Hoe
Shovel, for spreading compost
Spade or rotary cultivator
Rake
Water-fillable roller
Seed spreader (optional)

Ingredients
Existing lawn
Maiden grasses (*Miscanthus sinensis*) or
    fountain grasses (*Pennisetum
    alopecuroides*) for planting around
    house foundation (optional)
Narcissus bulbs, a good naturalizing culti-
    var, 3 per 1 square foot of arc shape
    (see text)
Small grasses, such as blue oat grass
    (*Helictotrichon sempervirens*) for plant-
    ing in entrance paving (optional)

For a lawn from seed
Lawn seed (see text); amount depends on
    mix
Compost or manure, 1¾ cubic feet per 1
    square yard
Lawn-starter fertilizer
Lime or sulfur if needed

Maintenance
Mow grass path frequently
Mow rest of lawn occasionally
Water lawn and path frequently
Water ornamental grasses (optional)
    regularly until established, then less
    frequently
Aerate and dethatch path in spring or
    early fall
Fertilize lawn and path from spring
    through fall

soil tested, and ask how much lime or sulfur to add to correct the soil for a lawn. Cultivate the area to a depth of 6 inches. Rake and roll the area until it is firm and either flat or gently contoured (bumps and dips will catch in the mower).

Sow the seed at the recommended rate either by hand or with a wheeled seeder. Rake the area very lightly, spread a thin layer of compost across it, not deep enough to completely cover the soil, and roll with a water-filled roller (half filled will be fine). Water thoroughly and frequently (perhaps as often as three times a day) to keep the lawn surface constantly moist until the seeds germinate. Continue to water regularly until the lawn is established.

PINK VENUS BED, GRASS STRIP

To keep the lawn showcase green and manicured from the house all the way to the fence, it once had to be irrigated, mowed, fertilized, edged, aerated, thatched, reseeded, protected from birds, weeded, chemically treated—every kind of coddling all year long. The tyranny is over now. The Venus garden took away two-thirds of the grass. Pale and rosy pink flowers bloom here instead: oxalis flutes, ragged daisy faces, giant spiked allium globes, sagging velvet roses. The fence is ribboned in pink clematis, the strawberry tree with a trouble-free Lady Banks' rose.

HOW TO DO IT ≋ This path is cut from an existing lawn and edged with wooden benderboard. To start a grass path from seed, see page 86; to lay one with rolls of turf, see page 108.

Mark out the path perimeter with the twine and stakes. Make the path about half as wide as the border. A straight path looks fitting next to the straight lines of a house. If you prefer a curved path, keep the curves shallow, build out the foundation plantings so they don't follow the lines of the house so clearly, and obscure the hard faces of the house or the fence with an occasional tree or shrub or vines. Consider the points of access onto the path; if they are narrow, place a few stepping-stones to protect the turf.

With the edger, define the path edge along the twine, slicing deeply into the turf. Stand on the flower bed side of the line, so as not to wear down the new path. If you're removing a large area of turf for the flower bed, rent a sod cutter from an equipment rental yard. For small areas, remove the grass with a sharp, straight-edged spade, scalping and rolling it off the soil.

Lay edging along the sides of the path to help prevent the grass from encroaching into the flower bed. Two layers of redwood or cedar benderboard make a simple barrier. First straighten the path edge with the spade, and pull soil back from the edge, so there's a clean 4-inch-deep trench for the edging. Position the benderboard in the trench, two layers thick, staggering the layers and nailing them together. Hammer the stake one-by-twos alongside them, in the flower bed, at intervals of 4 feet. Nail the benderboard to the stakes so that it protrudes 1 inch above the path. Firm the soil against the outside of the edging. Saw off any protruding stakes flush with the edging.

Prepare the soil for planting. Dig in plenty of manure or compost. Plant the lamb's ears along both sides of the path, 4 inches from the edge and 12 inches apart to fill in quickly and spill over the edging. Plant the flower beds with your choice of pink-flowering plants and a scattering of white- and blue-flowering ones for contrast.

Inexpensive
Easy
Location: Sun or very light shade

Tools
Measuring tape
Twine and stakes
Half-moon lawn edger
Straight-edged spade, or sod cutter for large area
Hammer
Saw
Planting trowel
Hose or watering can

Ingredients
Stepping-stones (optional)
Redwood or heartwood cedar benderboard for edging, two layers, length of path perimeter, and nails
Stake one-by-twos, 12 inches long, 1 stake per 4 feet of perimeter
Manure or compost, 1½ to 3 cubic feet per 1 square yard of flower bed
Lamb's ears (Stachys byzantina), 1 per 1 foot of border
Pink-flowering plants, such as roses, English daisies (Bellis perennis, pink double), spotted nettles (Lamium maculatum), globe alliums (Allium schubertii), oxalis
White- and blue-flowering plants, such as nicotiana (Nicotiana alata) or columbine (Aquilegia spp.)

Maintenance
Water path frequently
Water plants regularly
Mow path regularly
Fertilize path from spring through fall
Aerate and dethatch path in spring or early fall
Replace patches of path in spring, if necessary

SAWDUST SLOPE AND GERANIUMS

Every yard of sawdust path in this hillside geranium garden has its slipping point and angle of repose. Where the gradient gets too steep, wooden cleats hold the path steady, or the path is routed back across the slope, then turned gently down and round, leaving an offshoot trail, like a runaway truck exit, that dead-ends at a bench on the flat.

The sawdust is soft and deep; footprints dent it. When the rain drips down through the birch trees, the path smells of cut logs in a woodpile and gets spongy, but not slippery. After a winter of rains, most of last spring's fresh sawdust has washed over and down the bank and in among the plants, where it improves the native clay. The new sawdust arrives fragrant and orange. After you spread it out and tamp it down, the path returns gradually to a superrich brown. You put the clay drainpipes on the path corners so you can rub the scented geraniums in them as you pass, you push the cleats in, and every yard is firm for another year.

HOW TO DO IT ⌇⌇⌇ This path is laid directly on top of the soil and relaid each spring, after the winter rains but in time to catch one or two showers, which will help compact the sawdust. There is no edging; the sawdust washes into surrounding plantings during heavy rains.

Clear any weeds, and rake the ground level. On a slope, make the path surface a little lower on the downslope side, so that water will drain freely off the path. On the inside of the slope, cut a neat edge into the bank. Make the path 3 feet wide where possible, narrower on tight corners or around trees.

Spread 2 inches of sawdust over the ground, dampen it, and compact it with the tamper or roller. Spread another 2 inches of sawdust over the first layer, dampen it, and compact it. Rake it level. Dig cleats into any steep parts of the path, so that only the narrow edges show.

The path will wear down through the year. If it doesn't wash into the neighboring planting beds, consider shoveling some of it there, as mulch, before laying the new sawdust in spring. Or let the path build up a little each year so that it drains more readily.

Place the clay drainpipes at path intersections. Fill them with potting soil to within 2 inches of the rim, and plant the scented-leaved geraniums inside. Plant hardy geraniums and other shade-loving plants alongside the path. For drama, be sure to plant a few of the giant magenta geraniums *(Geranium maderense).*

Inexpensive
Easy
Location: Light shade

Tools
Rake
Straight-edged spade, for cutting path
    edge
Measuring tape
Shovel, for spreading sawdust
Hose
Hand-held tamper or water-fillable roller
Planting trowel

Ingredients
Sawdust, ground, from local lumber mill,
    3 cubic feet per 1 square yard of path
Cleats (if necessary), pieces of two-by-
    four, width of path
Clay drainpipes
Potting soil
Scented geraniums *(Pelargonium* spp.,
    fragrant-leaved kind), 1 per drainpipe
Hardy geraniums *(Geranium* spp., includ-
    ing *G. maderense),* foxgloves *(Digitalis
    purpurea),* forget-me-nots *(Myosotis
    sylvatica),* coral bells *(Heuchera san-
    guinea),* brunneras *(Brunnera macro-
    phylla),* violets *(Viola* spp.), wood
    anemones *(Anemone nemorosa)*

Maintenance
Water plants regularly
Rake path for a fresh look, as desired
Lay new sawdust annually

ROOM WITH RAILROAD TIES

There's a small room here, defined by five railroad ties. It has no ceiling and no walls to speak of—except a pair of giant phormiums that cut off the view to the house—but it has an entry-way from the lawn over a threshold of stepping-stones, views out into the garden, and a set of small furnishings: a 20-inch-tall urn, a rusty chair with a 15-inch-square seat, and collections of pebbles and fine-textured small plants.

So as to invite you in, the flooring is boldly patterned and wide enough for full-scale feet. Once you're over the threshold, the way forward turns past the chair to the picture window, so to speak—with an intimate, behind-the-scenes view into the backs of the flower beds bordering the lawn and on through to a small, vine-covered potting shed.

HOW TO DO IT ❧❧❧

The railroad ties are laid directly on top of compacted soil, without a foundation. They are so heavy they are unlikely to shift in any kind of soil, but if your soil drains very badly, lay 4 inches of crushed rock or gravel below the ties. Choose the ties carefully; many are soaked with tar, which will ooze in hot weather and track around the garden. Ask friends to help you carry and position the ties.

Clear any weeds, and rake the ground level. Mark out the room perimeter with the twine and stakes. Make it approximately 8 feet wide (check the length of your railroad ties; most are about 8 feet) and 5 feet long.

Dig a trench the length and width of the room, as deep as the railroad ties (about 6 inches). Firm the bottom of the trench with the back of the spade or the tamper. Place the level across the piece of two-by-four to check that the trench floor is level; once the first railroad tie is in the trench, it will be difficult to rework the base. Position the ties in the trench, broad sides up, 4 inches apart.

Fill the strips between the ties with a mix of soil and sand, to within ½ inch of the surface. Tamp down the mix with the trowel. Plant the carpet bugles, 6 inches apart, in the strips, and water thoroughly; they'll flower in blue spikes in early summer. For a less strongly patterned effect, plant a few baby's tears among the carpet bugles and perhaps bellflowers or a cluster of small succulents.

For the threshold (optional), dig a trench 4 inches deep, lay 2 inches of sand, dampen and tamp it, and lay the stepping-stones onto the sand. Settle them with the mallet.

To break up the strong rectangle of the room and turn it into a more alluring L-shape, designer Suzanne Porter placed the chair in one corner and next to it a large pot and a pile of pebbles. Kitty-corner from the chair, the urn pulls you into the room from the lawn; any focal point will do. To keep things in scale, furnish the room with small objects and small, fine-textured plants.

Inexpensive
Easy
Location: Sun or light shade

Tools
Rake
Measuring tape
Twine and stakes
Straight-edged spade
Hand-held tamper (optional)
Level
Planting trowel
Hose or watering can
Rubber mallet, for threshold (optional)

Ingredients
5 railroad ties
Builder's sand, 2½ cubic feet for strips, plus
    ½ cubic foot for threshold (optional)
Carpet bugles (*Ajuga reptans*), 16 per 1
    strip between ties
Baby's tears (*Soleirolia soleirolii*) (optional)
Bellflowers (*Campanula portenschlagiana*)
    (optional)
Hen and chicks (*Echeveria elegans*)
    (optional)
4 stepping-stones, for threshold (optional)
Small-scale objects for furniture
Fine-textured, airy, and small-flowered
    plants, such as grasses, coreopsis, coral
    bells (*Heuchera*), columbine
    (*Aquilegia*), small filipendula

Maintenance
Water plants regularly

CONCRETE

Finished smooth, concrete sparkles in sun and moonlight. It makes a beautifully luminous line through a grove of white-trunked trees, such as jacquemontii birch. The expansion joints repeat at rhythmic intervals, marking off the curves, as the path slinks through the trees. Sunbeams that pierce the trees bounce straight off the white surface, creating glimmering pools of refracted light in the shadows.

Designers working in the Japanese style often choose concrete to draw out an abstract paving pattern on the ground. They mold it into slim bars or huge squares, leave it plain and stark or seed it with pretty gray or beige gravels. The patterns change to mark movement from one part of the garden to another.

Concrete is a natural material for play. It takes color and almost any shape. The surface can be studded, stamped, brushed, engraved. There are colors like stone and pigments that suggest marble and frames to stamp shapes of cobble, but trying to mimic expensive natural materials is perhaps the least satisfying kind of play and likely to be the least successful unless you're a good artist.

A jack-hammered concrete patio provides imaginative opportunities for paving. Lay the large chunks as stepping-stones, then emphasize the ruin theme by wedging cornice (from a salvage yard) into the flower beds, making sure it tilts as if it just fell. A piece of unabashedly imitation classical column (the sort that holds up glass tables) might make a beautiful seat. Garden designer Tom Chakas adds rebar for vine supports and airy sculpture, concrete footings for pathside water bowls.

Most concrete slabs and pavers are not too heavy to move about, but making and pouring concrete is strenuous work. Go at it slowly, making a couple of pavers a day, or ask friends to help. Tackle it only if you have had experience or you're the sort of person who won't be terribly disappointed if a paver or two cracks or an edge crumbles. Commercially manufactured precast pavers last longer than homemade concrete, but cracks invariably appear even in professionally poured paths. Concrete paths are especially prone to cracking in very cold climates.

GRAVEL-SEEDED BARS, PEBBLE FILL

Bar after bar of hard-angled concrete marches from an entrance court down the side of the house to the front door, across a background of smooth-washed pebbles. To signal people onto the path and up to the door, which is out of sight, the start of the path announces itself in a constructivist swirl of long and short bars and zigzagging angles.

Concrete pours into almost any shape, and you can seed the wet surface with almost any material you please. Pretty river gravel speckles these bars with black, white, gray, brown, and slate blue. The colors harmonize with the gray house walls and the gray gravel entrance court. The blue matches the blue of the pebbles, which spill out between the concrete bars into the garden.

HOW TO DO IT ❊❊❊

These 4-inch-thick bars are made by hand, from dry materials mixed on site and poured into hand-built wooden forms. Gravel is seeded into the surfaces of the bars, and pebbles are laid between the bars. The path rests on a foundation of 4 inches of gravel, a firm, long-lasting base for most situations. In a frost-free climate and freely draining soil, you could lay just 2 inches of gravel; if your soil freezes hard or drains poorly, lay 8 inches. (In very frosty areas, consider using concrete that includes an air-entraining agent; you'll need to hire a power mixer to mix it properly.)

Before you start, draw out a plan on graph paper, so you know how many forms you'll need and how much of each material to order. Make the path 4½ feet wide (the bars are 4 feet long; the extra inches are for the forms), and work out the length in units of 2 feet (the bars are 18 inches wide and the gaps between them 6 inches). For the standard bars, you can make just two forms and reuse them four hours after pouring when the bars are set, thus building the path in increments; or you can build a form for every bar and pour the path without a rest. Any extra-long bars or multi-angled threshold stones will require their own forms, designed to suit your space.

Clear any weeds, and rake the ground level. Mark out the path perimeter with the twine and stakes.

Dig an 8-inch trench the length and width of the path. Firm the bottom of the trench if you've disturbed the soil while digging. Spread 2 inches of gravel into the bottom of the trench. Moisten this layer, and pack down the surface with the tamper or roller. Lay the next 2 inches in the same way. Check with the level that the gravel bed is even.

Working outside the trench, make the forms for the concrete. For each form, cut two 18-inch pieces of two-by-four and two 52-inch pieces. Place the long sides so that they overlap the short ones; the inside of the form needs to measure 4 feet by 18 inches. Nail the corners, two nails per corner. Make the forms sturdy; concrete is heavy and will push apart flimsy joints.

Position the forms in the trench, allowing 2 inches between the forms, so that when you remove the forms, the gaps will be 6 inches wide. Drive the stakes into the soil to secure the forms; place them against the forms, 6 inches from each corner, 8 stakes per form. Check that the forms are still parallel to each other and spaced equidistantly.

Make the screed you'll need to level the concrete. Set the 30-inch length of two-by-four on edge across one of the forms, with 4 inches protruding on

Moderately inexpensive
Moderately difficult
Location: Sun or light shade

Tools
Graph paper and pencil
Rake
Measuring tape
Twine and stakes
Straight-edged spade, for digging
Shovel, for spreading materials
Hose
Hand-held tamper, or water-fillable roller
Level
Saw
Hammer
Paintbrush, for applying releasing agent
Rubber gloves
Concrete-mixing bucket, at least 4-cubic-foot capacity
Hoe
Edger, for finishing concrete edges
Wooden float, small
Stiff nylon broom
Plastic sheet or wet cloths, if weather turns wet or hot
Planting trowel

Ingredients
Gravel, sharp-edged, for the foundation, ⅛- or ¼-inch, 5 cubic feet per 1 yard of path
For each standard form:
    12 feet of two-by-four
    8 double-headed nails
    8 stake one-by-twos, 12 inches long
For the screed:
    Piece of two-by-four 30 inches long
    1-inch nails
    Piece of plywood 17½ inches long, ½ inch thick, 3 or 4 inches wide
Commercial releasing agent
Bags of dry ready-mix concrete without lime, approx. 2 cubic feet per bar
Smooth, varicolored river gravel for seeding concrete surface, approx. ¼ cubic foot per bar
Blue pebbles for fill, 1 cubic foot per strip
Gray plants: lamb's ears (*Stachys byzantina*), wormwood (*Artemisia* 'Powis Castle')

Maintenance
Water plants regularly until established, then less frequently

either side. To the two-by-four, nail the 17½-inch piece of plywood so that it extends ½ inch down into the form. As you pull the two-by-four across the top of a form, the plywood edge will level the concrete ½ inch below the top.

With the paintbrush, grease the insides and tops of the forms with the commercial releasing agent, so that you'll be able to slip the forms up easily off the concrete bars when they're set.

Put on the rubber gloves to keep the cement off your skin. In the bucket, prepare the concrete according to the directions on the bag. Make enough for just two forms, approximately 4 cubic feet, so that you have time to pour and float both bars before the concrete starts to harden. Add the water slowly, and turn the mix thoroughly; if the consistency is right (not too stiff, not runny), the finished pavers are less likely to crack or crumble.

Pour concrete into the first form, filling 1 foot at a time. If you have a helper, have him or her start spreading and packing the concrete with a hoe, tamping out any air bubbles and pressing the mix against the edges and into the corners. Fill the next foot, and so on to the end of the first form.

Level the concrete in the first form with your homemade screed. The surface of the concrete should be ½ inch lower than the top of the form, to allow for the layer of river gravel. Pull the screed along the top of the form in a sawing motion. Again tamp the corners and edges, then compact the edges further by running the edger between the form and the concrete. Don't press on the front tip of it or you'll make divots in the concrete.

Sprinkle a thin layer of river gravel over the wet surface of the bar. With the wooden float, press the gravel down into the concrete and smooth the surface by sliding the float over it. Pour the second form, pack and level the concrete, and add the gravel to its surface.

If you are going to wait for the first bars to set and reuse the forms, wash the concrete off your tools now. Watch the bars; as the concrete begins to harden, brush the surface with the broom to expose the gravel, and, with a very gentle spray from the hose, wash the gravel clean.

Remove the forms three or four hours after you poured the bars. Leave the bars to cure for five days. Cover them with the plastic sheet if it starts to rain. Cover them with the wet cloths if the weather turns hot and dry.

When the bars are all cured, fill the gaps between the bars with the blue pebbles. Plant gray-foliaged plants to pick up the soft color in the concrete.

PATH OF RIGHTEOUSNESS

On Sunday afternoons, when sculptor Marcia Donahue's small urban jungle garden doubles as an art gallery, people step off the gravel terrace onto one of the overgrown paths and lose themselves, ducking under tree branches, brushing through screens of bamboo, tiptoeing around the thumb of a hand-shaped pond, whispering about the china teacups in the treetops, and musing over the inscription on this path of concrete triangles embedded with horseshoes and edged with bowling balls.

Among so much whimsy, why the Path of Righteousness? "Have you never wondered where you might find it?" she teased. "I like to have what I'm looking for right here in my garden."

HOW TO DO IT ⟨⟨⟨ These pavers are made by hand from dry
concrete mix and laid directly on top of the soil without a foundation. They
may shift and tilt naturally, and perhaps crack. If your soil freezes or drains
poorly, lay 4 inches of gravel and 2 inches of sand below the pavers.

Play with the idea of changing the paver shapes and using different objects.
By the time you read this, Marcia will probably have changed hers.

Make the pavers in batches of three, so there's time to hand-shape each one
while the mix is still malleable (about an hour). On a firm, flat surface, lay the
sheet of plastic to work on. With a marker or a piece of chalk, draw the shapes
for three pavers. Marcia made triangles, roughly 20 by 20 by 30 inches, but you
can make any shape—just keep in mind that sharp angles in concrete are apt
to crack. Marcia's path is roughly 20 inches wide.

Arrange the horseshoes, or whatever items you've chosen, in the chalked
shape, placing them face down on the plastic. Put on rubber gloves to keep the
cement off your skin. In the bucket or wheelbarrow, make the concrete by
adding water according to the instructions on the bag. Shovel the concrete
mix onto the chalk shapes. With the trowel, tamp the concrete to remove any
air pockets, level it to 3 inches thick, and mold the sides into smooth edges.
Leave it to set for several hours.

As soon as the concrete has set, turn the pavers over carefully and clean the
horseshoes with the wet sponge. If the surface isn't completely stiff, you can
brush it vigorously with the nylon brush to get a rough look. If you like, etch
words or markings into the pavers with a file, screwdriver, or electric grinder.
Move the pavers off the plastic work sheet, and leave them to cure for five days
in a shady area. Cover them with the plastic sheeting if it starts to rain. Cover
them with the wet cloths if the weather turns hot and dry.

Mark out the perimeter of the path with the twine and stakes. Dig a 3-inch
trench the width and length of the path, piling the soil on one side of the path
to make the bank. Rake the trench level. Settle the pavers into the dirt path,
moistening the dirt to get a good fit. Leave 4-inch gaps between pavers, and fill
these either with bare soil, as Marcia has, or with a ground cover such as blue
star creeper or moss, or with pebbles or marbles or whatever strikes you as
interesting.

Pile the bowling balls, or any pleasing objects, onto the bank. Plant between the objects with small, unusually colored plants like black lily turf. For
a jungle experience, plant bamboo, trees, or shrubs alongside the path.

Inexpensive
Moderately easy
Location: Sun or shade

Tools
Plastic work sheet, approx. 6 by 8 feet
Marker or chalk
Rubber gloves
Concrete-mixing bucket or wheelbarrow
Hose or watering can
Builder's trowel, rectangular
Household sponge, for cleaning horse-
    shoes
Stiff nylon brush (optional)
File, screwdriver, or electric grinder
    (optional)
Plastic sheeting or wet cloths, if weather
    turns wet or hot
Twine and stakes
Straight-edged spade, for digging
Rake
Planting trowel

Ingredients
Horseshoes, 1 or 2 per paver, or other
    items to embed, such as tiles, thick
    glass, pebbles, or china
Bags of all-purpose concrete mix, approx.
    3 cubic feet per 8 pavers
Bowling balls, approx. 6 per 1 yard of path,
    or other objects for bank beside path
Small plants with unusual forms or colors,
    such as black lily turf (*Ophiopogon
    planiscapus* 'Nigrescens'), approx. 5 per
    1 yard of path; in very cold winter cli-
    mates, grow a hardier alternative

Maintenance
Water plants regularly

WHITE SQUARES, BLUE RIBBONS

The hillside is still with heat most of the year. Even in the shade of the eucalyptus and oaks, the air stays heavy. Stepping off the bubbling asphalt into this entrance, you arrive at an oasis. The walk is cool and blue and refreshingly simple to look at. Smooth, white, concrete pavers bleached by the sun rest among ribbons of blue fescue grass; giant blue agave rosettes lope toward the light; little sticks of blue kleinia poke through the grass. All year, with almost no maintenance, these plants hold their cool blueness. From spring through fall, 6-foot pencil-thin spikes of kangaroo flowers cast crisp shadows onto the bright white wall.

HOW TO DO IT ❋❋❋

Precast pavers are laid on a foundation of 4 inches of gravel and 2 inches of sand, a firm, long-lasting base suitable for most situations. If your soil freezes hard or drains poorly, lay 4 inches of crushed rock (1½-inch), 2 inches of gravel, and 2 inches of sand. In a frosty climate, develop a different planting design; these plants create a cool atmosphere, and they're too tender for frosty climates. The path has no edging; if your path is on unstable soil or slopes, install a metal or benderboard edging (see page 59) to contain the path base. The pavers are heavy; ask someone to help you or hire help for the afternoon.

(In the run from the street and driveway to the front door, landscape architect Susan Van Atta used strips of unglazed pale blue tile set in mortar instead of the fescues, which people could conceivably trip over. The gaps were filled with wet mortar and the tile tapped into it while wet. Where safety is paramount, the pavers could also be set end to end, without gaps.)

Clear any weeds, and rake the ground level. Mark out the path perimeter with the twine and stakes; make it two pavers (6 feet) wide for a comfortable entrance path, plus 4 inches for the grass strip in the center.

Dig a 9-inch trench the length and width of the path; firm the bottom of the trench if you've disturbed the soil while digging. Spread 2 inches of gravel into the bottom of the trench. Moisten this layer, and pack down the surface with the tamper or roller. Lay the next 2 inches in the same way. On top of the gravel, lay 2 inches of sand. Dampen the sand, tamp it, level it, and tamp again. Check with the level that the sand bed is even.

In one corner, lay the first paver against the twine. Maneuver it into place as gently as you can so as not to make deep treads in the sand bed. With the level, check that it's sitting flat; if necessary, lift the paver and spread sand underneath it.

Lay the second paver alongside the first, leaving a 4-inch space for the fescues. Try to keep the sand bed even, as you work. Add sand to fill dips, and pull the piece of two-by-four in a sawing motion across the bed to level it. Retamp, and check with the level as necessary.

When the last paver is in place, fill the gaps with a mix of sand and soil to within ½ inch of the path surface. Tamp the mix firmly with the trowel. Plant the blue fescues in the gaps, 8 inches apart. Plant the agaves and the kleinias around and up to the path edge. Plant the kangaroo paws and the paperbark tree behind them.

Moderately inexpensive
Moderately easy
Location: Sun

Tools
Rake
Measuring tape
Twine and stakes
Straight-edged spade, for digging
Shovel, for spreading materials
Hose
Hand-held tamper or water-fillable roller
Level, 6-foot
Piece of straight two-by-four, 6 feet long
Planting trowel

Ingredients
Gravel, sharp-edged, ⅝- or ¾-inch, 6½ cubic feet per 1 yard of path
Builder's sand, 3½ cubic feet per 1 yard of path
Pavers, smooth finish, 3 feet square, 3 inches thick, 2 per 1 yard of path
Blue fescues (*Festuca ovina* 'Glauca'), small plants in flats, 5 per 1 yard of strip between pavers
Border plants: blue agave (*Agave attenuata* 'Nova'), kleinia (*Senecio serpens* 'Chalksticks'), kangaroo paws (*Anigozanthos flavidus*), paperbark tree (*Melaleuca quinquenervia* or *M. leucadendra*)

Maintenance
Water sparingly, except for kangaroo paws, which need more water during flowering
Remove spent flowering stems from kangaroo paws to encourage more flowers

SCULPTED CONCRETE STROLL GARDEN

In the Lennettes' Industrial Oasis, created by artist and garden designer Harland Hand, a path of soft-edged sculpted concrete unfolds into an exquisitely choreographed stroll garden. The city lot is small, but the journey is a long one, slowed by curves in the path, sitting areas where the walkway widens occasionally into a terrace, a pond at the farthest point, and, all the way out through the changing vistas, one-of-a-kind plants that stop you in your tracks—on New Year's Day, licorice-black aeoniums and lime echeverias, one lemon jonquil, a patch of candy-pink oxalis.

Four thousand different plants inhabit this garden. The generous, pale, concrete stones, shaped individually and smeared with pigments that pick up the pinks and grays in the plantings, unify it into a wonderland of soft, reflected light and pictorial color.

HOW TO DO IT ⬦⬦⬦

These concrete stones are made by hand from dry materials mixed together and sculpted while wet directly on top of the soil, without a foundation. Dry pigments are smeared onto the drying surface. If your soil freezes or drains poorly, lay 8 inches of gravel below the stones.

Clear any weeds, and rake the ground level. Mark out the path perimeter with the twine and stakes. Make the width generous, at least 3 feet. Start at the far end of the path, drawing a large, elliptical shape in the dirt with a stick. Since the path probably ends here at a destination—a bench or a view or a doorway—consider creating an extra-large terrace stone or threshold stone to mark this point. Harland's stones vary; no two are the same, but many are 26 to 30 inches wide and 22 to 26 inches long. In the terraces, one or two stones measure about 4 feet wide. All are elliptical.

Put on the rubber gloves to keep the cement off your skin. In the bucket or wheelbarrow, thoroughly combine the dry materials for the concrete—1 part cement, 4 parts sand, 1 part pea gravel. Measure the materials in level shovelfuls. Start by making enough concrete for one or two stones. Once the mix is uniform, add water gradually, turning and mixing as you go until it's "a little wetter than sand for sand castles," says Harland. If the mix becomes too wet, leave it for an hour.

Shovel the concrete onto the marked area. With the trowel, tamp and smooth it into a stone about 3 inches thick. With your hands, taper the edges so that when soil covers them the stone will seem to rise naturally from bedrock.

Draw the next shape in the dirt, leaving a planting gap of about 4 inches at the closest point between the stones. Space and change the sizes of the stones so that they make a pleasing rhythm to lead the eye. Keep to generous elliptical shapes; small stones will destroy the quiet sequence of forms and make the path crazy-looking.

Before the concrete sets, on each stone smear and trowel into the surface a little umber pigment mixed with a handful of dry cement and then a little black pigment mixed with a handful of dry cement. Leave the surface somewhat rough so that it's less slippery in wet weather. Wash the concrete off the tools before it dries.

Wait five days for the concrete to cure. Cover the stones with the plastic

Inexpensive
Moderately easy
Location: Sun or light shade

Tools
Rake
Measuring tape
Twine and stakes
Stick, to draw shapes in dirt
Rubber gloves
Concrete-mixing bucket or wheelbarrow
Shovel or hoe, for mixing concrete
Hose or watering can
Builder's trowel, rectangular, for sculpting
Plastic sheet or wet cloths, if weather
    turns wet or hot
Planting trowel

Ingredients
For 2 stones, approx. 24 by 28 inches,
    approx. 2½ cubic feet of concrete,
    composed of
        1 part cement
        4 parts builder's sand
        1 part pea gravel
Small bag of umber pigment
Small bag of black pigment
Weed-free topsoil, or potting soil, to fill
    between stones
Gray plants: lamb's ears (Stachys byzantina), snow-in-summer (Cerastium tomentosum), blue fescue (Festuca ovina 'Glauca'), hen and chicks (Echeveria elegans)
Green plants: mondo grass (Ophiopogon japonicus), Scotch moss (Sagina subulata), periwinkle (Vinca minor)

Maintenance
Water most plants regularly until established, then less frequently
Water Scotch moss and mondo grass regularly, even when established
Trim and thin plants so that no one species becomes invasive
Let stones accumulate moss, algae, and cracks

sheet if it starts to rain. Cover them with the wet cloths if the weather turns hot and dry.

Bring in a wheelbarrowful of the topsoil or potting soil, and fill in the spaces between and around the stones for planting. Plant anything low-growing—miniature bulbs, moss, dwarf grasses, creepers—but keep the Harland look by including many gray-foliaged plants with soft textures, to take the chill look off the concrete, and contrasting strips of dark green plants, to accentuate the lines of the stones.

CHESSBOARD WALK

The natural stone walkways elsewhere in this garden leave the eye free to drift out over the trees to the valley below or up across a ridge where wild turkeys graze. Here at the chessboard, concrete pavers are lined up in a bold pattern against the grass, and on them rests a sculpture collection that's more arresting than the view. The art draws you out into the soft grass, around the rusty iron castles with flags on the turrets anchoring the corners, past the tall kings with dew dripping from their metal robes, and down the harlequin corridor between the opposing rows of armored, battle-ready pawns. The mind turns away from the landscape and loses itself in play.

HOW TO DO IT ❊❊❊

This chessboard is made of grass strips, laid as turf (sod), and precast concrete pavers, half of them stained or purchased in a contrasting color, to make a checkerboard, laid on a foundation of 2 inches of sand. The pavers sit flush with the turf so the board can be mowed. In soils that freeze hard, the pavers will heave and need some resettling in spring. If your soil is often soggy, improve the drainage with organic matter before laying the sand. Because turf dries out and spoils quickly, be sure to have the pavers laid and the soil prepared before taking delivery of the turf. In hot weather, sprinkle the turf pile to keep it fresh and ask at least one friend to help cut the turf while you roll out the strips. To grow the grass from seed, see page 86.

Stain half of the pavers, unless you've bought pavers in contrasting colors. Brush off the surface of each paver, rinse it with water, and while it's still damp, apply the stain with the paintbrush. Try to avoid streaks, but don't worry too much about uneven coloring or mottling. Set the pavers aside to dry.

Clear any weeds, and rake the ground level. Mark out the board perimeter with the twine and stakes, 14 feet x 4 inches square, and then the surrounding grass path, 3 feet wide.

Dig a 3-inch trench the length and width of the chessboard; leave the surrounding path area undisturbed for now. Firm the bottom of the trench if you've disturbed the soil while digging. Spread 2 inches of sand into the trench, dampen it, and roll it with the roller. Rake it level, and roll it again. With the level on top of the piece of one-by-eight, check that the sand bed is even.

In one corner, lay the first paver against the twine, perfectly square. Place it on top of the sand, without disturbing the sand bed, if possible, and settle it by tapping it with the mallet. Lay the second paver alongside the first, leaving a 4-inch gap for the grass strip. Alternate the paver colors. Try to keep the sand bed even as you work. Add sand to fill dips, and pull the piece of two-by-four in a sawing motion across the bed to level it. Reroll, and level as necessary.

When the last paver is in place on the first line, check the alignment of the pavers carefully, and remeasure the gaps. Also check that the pavers are level, using the level across the one-by-eight.

Lay the second row of pavers, light square alongside dark square, with a 4-inch gap between the rows. Work from a knee pad on the sand bed. At the end of the second row, check the alignment, and remeasure the gaps. Complete the chessboard by laying eight rows of pavers.

Moderately inexpensive
Moderately difficult
Location: Sun or very light shade

Tools
Brush, to clean pavers
Hose
Paintbrush, 4-inch, for applying stain to pavers
Rake
Measuring tape
Twine and stakes
Straight-edged spade, for digging
Shovel, for spreading sand
Water-fillable roller
Level
Piece of one-by-eight, 6 feet long
Rubber mallet
Piece of two-by-four, 4 feet long
Knee pad
Planting trowel
Sharp knife, for cutting turf

Ingredients
64 plain square pavers, smooth finish, 18 inches square, 1 inch thick
Concrete stain, terra-cotta color, to paint on 32 pavers
Builder's sand, 37½ cubic feet, for chessboard
High-phosphate lawn-starter fertilizer
Compost, 1¼ cubic yards, for improving soil (optional)
Grass turf, 1-inch thick, 70 square feet for chessboard, plus 230 square feet for surrounding path; buy variety reliable in your area, from highest-quality supplier
Chess pieces

Maintenance
Water grass frequently
Mow grass regularly
Aerate and dethatch grass in spring or early fall
Fertilize from spring through fall
Resettle pavers in spring, if necessary

Prepare the strips between the pavers for the turf. Kneeling on the one-by-eight placed across several pavers, trowel the high-phosphate fertilizer (use the amount recommended on the label) into the strips, and cultivate to a depth of 4 or 5 inches, mixing the sand with the soil below. Try not to disturb the pavers. Tamp the soil with the trowel. Water the strips thoroughly.

Prepare the ground around the chessboard by removing 1 inch of topsoil and raking the ground level. (Spread the topsoil in another part of the garden.) If your soil drains poorly, remove an extra 2 inches, and spread a 2-inch layer of compost across the surface. The raked surface should be flush with the soil between the pavers. Cultivate the path area to a depth of 4 or 5 inches, mixing in high-phosphate fertilizer as you cultivate. Rake and roll the ground level. Water the area thoroughly.

Lay the turf for the grass path first, then do the strips between the pavers. Start at a corner of the chessboard, unrolling the first length of turf along the edge of the pavers on top of the moist soil (if the soil has dried, rewet it thoroughly). Lay the next length of turf right up against the end of the first, so that the edges are in firm contact, without gaps. At the end of the path, cut the turf with the sharp knife to fit. Lay another set of turf pieces alongside the first, cutting them to fit the width of the path and staggering the joints. Keep the edges pressed together so the turf won't dry out; don't stretch the turf. Complete the path around the chessboard.

Lay the strips of turf between the pavers in the same way: cut generous 4-inch-wide pieces to fit, and press the edges together, without gaps. If the turf completely fills the spaces between the pavers, the edges will not dry out quickly.

Roll the chessboard and the surrounding path with the roller. Water the whole area gently and thoroughly. The soil should be wet to a depth of at least 6 inches.

Until the turf is firmly rooted to the underlying soil, sprinkle it daily to keep it moist. Pay particular attention to the edges, because this is where the turf will dry out first. If gaps develop, pack them with soil. Avoid walking on the turf until it's established.

Place the chess pieces in position. If you like, improvise pieces from painted pots or rebar. This superb set was made by sculptor and landscape architect Jack Chandler.

DIAMOND PAVERS, WHITE FOXGLOVES

Street views from most of the houses on Madison Way are the same: the eye goes uninterrupted out across a perfect lawn, under the huge old southern magnolias that line both sides of the quiet street, up the neighbor's perfect lawn, and into the neighbor's window. This white-on-green billboard of foxgloves at the back of a corner lot traps the gaze in the garden. The diamond concrete pavers are a reminder to step out through the side gate and wander among the dozens of chest-high flower spikes swaying in the day-long shade.

HOW TO DO IT ≈≈≈

Each precast paver sits on a 2-inch bed of sand. The pavers will shift and heave over time but are easily resettled. If your soil freezes hard or drains poorly, lay 4 inches of crushed rock or gravel below the sand.

Clear any weeds, and rake the ground level. Lay out the pavers in a straight line, 6 inches between the tips. If you like, run a line of twine down the center of the path, and set each paver tip neatly on the line.

Mark around the edges of the pavers with the knife, then move the pavers off to the side. With the straight-edged spade, excavate to the depth of the paver plus 1 inch. The pavers will sit above the surrounding soil, so that they cast a shadow and look all the more dramatic; the height also keeps rain from sweeping soil over them.

Tamp the bottom of the first hole until the soil is firm and flat. Shovel 2 inches of sand on top of the soil, dampen it, and tamp it flat. Move the paver into position and gently settle it into the sand. Place each paver this way.

Plant the foxgloves in fall. They thrive in rich soil; improve poor soil with plenty of manure or compost. For a showy, eye-stopping mass of flowers, set them just 12 inches apart and run them right up to the path and under the window. In good soil and partial shade, if you leave some flower spikes on the plants long after they flower, so that the seed can ripen and drop, they will probably multiply.

For interest year round, plant a small, purple maple and tall ferns close to the house walls and periwinkles between the pavers (optional).

Foxglove flowers fit onto children's fingers like velvet gloves. Be watchful; every part of the plant is highly poisonous.

Inexpensive
Easy
Location: Light shade

Tools
Rake
Measuring tape
Twine and stakes (optional)
Knife, for marking outlines of pavers
Straight-edged spade, for digging
Hand-held tamper
Shovel, for spreading sand
Hose or watering can
Planting trowel

Ingredients
Pavers, 16 inches square, approx. 1 per 2 feet of path
Builder's sand, 1 cubic foot per 3 pavers
White foxgloves (*Digitalis* spp.), 9 per 1 square yard of planting area
Manure or compost, 2 cubic feet per 1 square yard, for improving soil (optional)
Maple (*Acer* spp.), small purple cultivar (optional)
Ferns (optional)
Periwinkles (*Vinca minor*) (optional)

Maintenance
Water plants regularly
Cut back foxglove flower stalks after flowering; new shoots may develop
Trim periwinkle (optional) away from pavers as necessary

CALCULATING QUANTITIES
OF MATERIALS

All the recipes in this book contain lists of ingredients that include the amounts of each material you'll need to build the path. The amounts are usually given for a yard of path and include an extra 10 percent in case of error. If you decide to make a deeper path base or a wider or narrower path, use the following information to calculate the amounts you'll need.

Loose materials, such as crushed rock, gravel, sand, and bark, are sold by the cubic foot. Multiply the width of the path, in feet, by the length of the path, in feet, and the depth of the material, also in feet; then add 10 percent for safety's sake. For example, for a path 4 feet wide and 20 feet long that requires a 2-inch layer of sand, you'd need 15 cubic feet of sand (4 x 20 x 0.17, plus 10 percent). That's more than half a cubic yard—divide cubic feet by 27 to convert to cubic yards.

Bricks are sold individually. They vary in size. For a path with joints between the bricks, you'll need about 4½ bricks per square foot, but to allow for some breakage and a small store for repairs, it's best to calculate on the basis of 5 bricks per square foot of path. Measure your path by multiplying the width, in feet, by the length, in feet. For a path 4 feet wide and 20 feet long, order 400 bricks (4 x 20 x 5).

Concrete and mortar are purchased by the cubic foot or cubic yard. Multiply the thickness of the concrete slab, in feet, by the width of the slab, in feet, by the length of the slab, in feet, then add 10 percent for error. For twenty concrete pavers 3 inches thick and 3 feet square, buy materials for 50 cubic feet of concrete (20 x 0.25 x 3 x 3, plus 10 percent). Divide by 27 to convert cubic feet to cubic yards.

If you're buying bags of ready-mix concrete or mortar, read the back of the bag to see how many bags you'll need. If you're mixing the ingredients from scratch, calculate the amounts of the individual materials as follows: add the part numbers together (for example, 1 part cement, 2 parts sand, 3 parts gravel = 6 parts), divide the total quantity of concrete, say 50 cubic feet, by that number (50 ÷ 6 = 8.33), then multiply each part by that number—8.33 cubic feet of cement, 16.67 cubic feet of sand, 25 cubic feet of gravel. Add 10 percent to each order.

Cut stone is sold by the square foot. Multiply the width of your path, in feet, by the length of your path, in feet. A path 6 feet wide and 21 feet long will require 126 square feet of stone. Decide on the size of the stones. If they'll be 18 inches square, you'll need 56 stones (1.5 x 1.5 = 2.25; 126 ÷ 2.25 = 56). If you're laying different-sized stones, make the pattern on graph paper and count up the number of each size.

Crazy paving, pieces of stone in irregular shapes, is estimated in square feet. Multiply the width of your path, in feet, by the length, in feet, and give that number to the supplier. He or she will help you estimate how many stones to start off with.

Fieldstone, quarried stone, and pebbles are often sold by weight. Measure the path area you want to cover, or the length of the path perimeter you want to edge, and ask the supplier to help estimate what you'll need. Or buy a small amount, lay it out in the path, and calculate from there.

Special slabs and boulders, for threshold stones or path markers, are often priced individually. Before you leave for the stone yard, decide how wide and long the slab must be to look special. Decide on the height of the boulder, and buy one at least one third larger so you can sink it into the ground for a natural effect.

GLOSSARY

Allée: a narrow walk bordered by trees or hedges

Benderboard: a wood edging in different thicknesses, inexpensive, somewhat flexible, and easy to install but not long-lasting unless it's redwood or heartwood cedar or treated

Brick set: a chisel-like tool with a 4-inch edge for cutting brick

Builder's sand: clean sand sold at building yards and home improvement centers for construction; not beach sand

Construction chalk: white powder sprinkled on the ground to mark out a path perimeter; twine and stakes are better for straight lines

Crazy paving: split stone slabs with irregular edges; fussy if pieces are small

Crowning: raising the center of a path above the sides, for drainage or aesthetic detail

Crushed rock, crushed stone: mechanically crushed, sharp-edged stone; packs well, makes an excellent path foundation

Cut stone: stone snap-cut or sawed into squares and rectangles; sawed stone has a sharper, cleaner edge than snap-cut stone

Decomposed granite, d.g.: naturally broken stone particles ranging in size from small gravel to sand

Drought-tolerant plant: a plant that thrives without regular water once established, but needs regular watering to get started

Fieldstone: natural stone from a hillside or field, unfinished

Fines, finings: dust from mechanical crushing of rock; creates a sandy texture in gravel and helps it pack down well

⅝-inch minus: stone crushed to ⅝-inch angular pieces and smaller with the crushing dust, or fines, added in; packs well, comfortable underfoot

Flagstone: stone split into random crazy paving slabs or into regular cut stone squares and rectangles; soft flagstone may stain easily and crack

Float: a flat piece of wood or steel with a handle, to smooth out the surface of concrete while it's wet

Foundation materials: layers of sharp-angled rock, or gravel, and sand that pack down well and provide a firm surface for brick, flagstone, stepping-stones, concrete pavers, or decorative gravels

Freely draining soil: soil through which water passes quickly after heavy rains; for a drainage test, see page 28

Gazebo: a garden building with a roof and open sides

Gravel: small stones crushed mechanically (angular edges) or collected from rivers or other natural deposits (round edges); see Crushed rock, Pea gravel

Mortar: a mix of cement, sand, either lime or fireclay, and water; for joints between bricks or pavers, apply as a dry mix (1 part cement, 4 parts sand, no lime or fireclay); sweep off any spills, and remove stains with a 10 percent solution of muriatic acid; for spot-mortaring paving to a foundation, make a wet mix (1 part cement, 3 parts sand, ½ part fireclay, and enough water to make it spreadable)

Parterre: a planting bed of herbs or flowers with a geometric pattern, often bordered with boxwood

Pea gravel, peastone: round stones suitable only for a path surface; will slide and roll and are therefore unsuitable for path foundations

Pergola: a series of columns or posts on either side of a path with wires or cross beams overhead, often covered in vines

Precast pavers: commercially manufactured pavers, usually concrete and extremely durable

Railroad tie: a heavy block of treated wood, approximately 8 feet by 8 inches by 6 inches

River rock, river stones: boulders worn smooth by water in rivers, for decorative use

Rootball: the ball of roots and the soil that clings to them when a plant is lifted from the ground or a pot

Sod: commercially grown turf, sold in carpetlike rolled strips, about 1 inch thick; should be moist and a beautiful healthy green; less environmentally friendly than growing a lawn from seed

Screed: a length of wood that's used to level sand or wet concrete

Shale: a fine-textured rock composed largely of consolidated clay or silt

Stabilizer: a trademarked natural product that binds tiny stone particles together, making a firm surface that is less prone to erosion

Stepping-stones: any kind of nonslippery stone, cut or uncut, set out in a string across lawn, gravel, or dirt; irregular, large, heavy stones make the most natural path

Tamp: to compact until firm, using the back of a shovel, a hand-held heavy tamping plate on a pole, a water-fillable drum roller, or a plate vibrator

Threshold stone: a large, attractive stepping-stone at the beginning or end of a path that makes a wide landing; also used at path intersections

Topsoil: fertile surface soil that contains organic matter; it takes centuries to build up over the infertile subsoil, so it shouldn't be buried

BIBLIOGRAPHY

The following books have inspired and informed my writing on paths:

Brookes, John. *John Brookes' Garden Design Workbook.* London: Dorling Kindersley, 1994.

Church, Thomas D., Grace Hall, and Michael Laurie. *Gardens Are for People.* Berkeley and Los Angeles: University of California Press, 1995.

Cooper, Guy, and Gordon Taylor. *Paradise Transformed: The Private Garden for the Twenty-first Century.* New York: The Monacelli Press, 1996.

Cotton, Lin. *All about Landscaping.* San Ramon, California: Ortho Books, 1980.

Crowe, Sylvia. *Garden Design.* Wappingers Falls, New York: Antique Collectors' Club, 1994.

Eck, Joe. *Elements of Garden Design.* New York: Henry Holt & Co., 1995.

Hayward, Gordon. *Garden Paths: Inspiring Designs and Practical Projects.* Charlotte, Vermont: Camden House Publishing, 1993.

Nierenberg, Ted, and Mark Kane. *The Beckoning Path: Lessons of a Lifelong Garden.* New York: Aperture, 1993.

Page, Russell. *The Education of a Gardener.* New York: HarperCollins Publishers, 1994.

Stevens, David. *The Garden Design Sourcebook: The Essential Guide to Garden Materials and Structures.* London: Conran Octopus, 1995.

Sunset Western Garden Book. Menlo Park, California: Sunset Publishing, 1995.

Taylor, Patrick. *The Garden Path.* New York: Simon & Schuster, 1992.

Treib, Marc, and Ron Herman. *A Guide to the Gardens of Kyoto.* Tokyo: Shufunotomo Co., 1980.

Walks, Walls, and Patio Floors. Menlo Park, California: Sunset Publishing, 1993.

Whitner, Jan Kowalczewski. *Stonescaping: A Guide to Using Stone in Your Garden.* Pownal, Vermont: Garden Way Publishing, 1992.

Wilkinson, Elizabeth, and Marjorie Henderson, eds. *Decorating Eden: A Comprehensive Sourcebook of Classic Garden Details.* San Francisco: Chronicle Books, 1992.

Yoshikawa, Isao. *Elements of Japanese Gardens.* Tokyo: Graphic-sha Publishing, 1990.

ACKNOWLEDGMENTS

I'm particularly grateful to the team of Chronicle Books staff and freelancers who put this book together so beautifully: editors Bill LeBlond and Leslie Jonath, designer David Bullen, design director Michael Carabetta, design coordinator Julia Flagg, copyeditor and dear friend Zipporah Collins, proofreader Carolyn Keating, and assistant editor Sarah Putman.

Many landscape architects and garden designers shared their time and their enthusiasms about garden paths with us, especially Heide Stolpestad Baldwin, Dan Borroff, Jack Chandler and Chris Moore, Topher Delaney and Andy Cochran, Marcia Donahue, Marta Fry, Sarah Hammond, Harland Hand, Ron Herman, Keeyla Meadows, Sharon Osmond, Robin Parer, Roger Raiche, Katie O'Reilly Rogers, Chris and Stephanie Tebbutt, Susan Van Atta, and Maggie Wych. Bill Gorgas, RG Turner Jr., and David Yakish, gardenmakers, kindly read the manuscript.

Thank you to all the people who opened their gardens to us for this book—we were greatly inspired by your paths and your hospitality. And, finally, for so much encouragement, thanks to Carol Henderson, David Goldberg, Pam Peirce, Jane Staw and colleagues, and again to Bill LeBlond.

GARDEN CREDITS

Gardens and garden owners are listed in roman type; the landscape architect or designer, in italics.
Pages 1, 7 (top, sleeping heads by Marcia Donahue), 16 (bottom), 30 (bottom), 36, 47, 48, 49, 50, (pots, furniture, fountain by Keeyla Meadows): *Keeyla Meadows;* pages 2, 100: *Marcia Donahue;* pages 4, 24: Lyngso Garden Materials, Inc.; pages 6, 12 (top), 104, 106: David Lennette, *Harland Hand;* pages 7 (bottom), 11, 23 (bottom), 35, 42, 43, 56: *Sarah Hammond;* pages 3, 8, 18, 94 (rebar sculpture by Tom Chakas): *Tom Chakas;* pages 10, 88, 89, 90, 91: *Robin Parer, Geraniaceae;* pages 12 (bottom), 20, 29 (bottom), 44, 46: *Sharon Osmond;* pages 13, 19, 26, 39, 41: Filoli Gardens; pages 16 (top), 23 (top), 27, 29 (top): Catherine Trefethen; pages 17 (top), 30 (top), 60, 62: Susan Pollock, Seattle, *Dan Borroff Landscape;* page 17 (bottom): *Harland Hand;* pages 21, 34, 63, 64: Scurlock residence, *Nancy Hammer Landscape Design;* pages 15, 22: Bloedel Reserve, Bainbridge Island, Washington; pages 28, 32, 66: Carl and Sharon Anduri residence, *Ron Herman, ASLA;* page 31: *John Denning, Brigitte Micmacker;* pages 33, 78, 79: William and Sheri Slater; pages 53, 55, 72: Molly and Richard Love, *Heide Stolpestad Baldwin;* pages 58, 75, 77: Costa and Julie Sevastopoulos, *Marta Fry Landscape Architects;* pages 69, 70, 71, 97, 99: *Isabelle C. Greene;* pages 80, 81: Robert and Mary Logan, *Susan Van Atta, ASLA;* page 82: Jeff and Virginia Mitchell, Beija-flor Resort and Gardens, *Stephanie Kotin and Christopher Tebbutt, Land & Place;* pages 85, 87: Scharffenberger Cellars, *Stephanie Kotin and Christopher Tebbutt, Land & Place;* pages 92, 93: *Suzanne Porter;* page 102: *Susan Van Atta, ASLA;* pages 107, 109 (sculpture by Jack Chandler): *Jack Chandler & Associates;* pages 110, 111: Barbara and Elliott Wolfe, *Delaney, Cochran, and Castillo.*

INDEX